In life there will always be obstacles, test and disappointments. If we are not careful our brokenness, can hinder or prevent us from reaching our goals. However, God has a solution to everything we face. Evangelist Annette Gatlin offers instructions, words of encouragement and Godly wisdom that helps us recover from our brokenness. She gives us testimony, scripture and prayers that help us realize that being repaired from brokenness is an inside job. This guide for healing the mind, body and soul is a joy to read. It brings hope for the hopeless, it brings joy to those who are sad, it reminds us that our conditions of brokenness are temporary.

Evangelist Gatlin through observation and experience provides insight on a plan for one's purpose. Too often we give up or give in. She reminds us to stay the course. Never give up, keep the faith and endure the process. She reminds us to pick up the pieces and move forward. It is about not allowing our brokenness to kill our dreams or distort our vision. For those who have been broken, strayed from the teachings and love of God, or those with health issues, broken relationships, lost jobs, and those who are living a life of destitute and isolation due to the pain of the past or present, this book can help in assisting individuals or families to getting back on track.

Rev. Dr. Roy Jones, Jr.
Published Author
Mentor - United Theological Seminary
Dayton, OH
Executive Minister
Saint Philip A.M.E. Church
240 Candler Road SE
Atlanta, GA 30317

***

Broken To Be Repaired is a magnificent guide to healing every aspect of your mind, body and spirit. It has been thoughtfully written by an evangelist who utilizes the Word of God and her own personal experiences to tap into the reader's innermost secret places where all of the hurts and pains of life are hidden to give useful instruction on how to perfect one's self and relationship not only with God but the world we live. The reader will refer to this book over again as a reference and reminder of how to successfully conquer the state of being broken during their healing process.

Attorney at Law
Memphis, Tennessee

***

They overcame Him by the blood of the lamb and the word of their testimony, (Revelation 12:11a).

One can only deliver or ascribe to writing such a liberating work such as this if they had not lived this out. There is no experience like personal experience. This God breathed work will bring much insight, healing, deliverance and breakthrough. It will breathe life into those who can relate and to those who may feel like they can not be set free. I have known Evangelist Annette (Fireball) Gatlin for a number of years. This Awesome Sold-out Soldier in the Lord is vital in this day and time when many professing Christ are turning away. This Phenomenal Woman is committed for life. I can truly say she understands suffering the trial of life and the benefits of the victories she's endured, conquered and overcome by God's undeniable Love for her.

Apostle Angela D. Thomas - Founder/CEO
By His Spirit World Mission
Facebook Angela Thomas

***

In this work, Evangelist Annette Hines-Gatlin offers the Blessings of Wholeness, Healing, and Hope. It is for those who knowingly and unknowingly need to find their way to the Power that is theirs to walk in. This is a must share, as it will Strengthen the Church, Heal Lives, and Transform the World.

Pastor Pierre L. Buie, MPA, CFI
Journey to Life International, Inc.
www.journeytolifeinternational.org

"Broken to be Repaired" can be equated to a cup of cold water that is refreshing for the soul. The book is transparent and sheds light for anyone in search of his or her purpose. It helps us to understand that God is with us throughout the process, which is enough to help us endure the process.

I met Annette Hines in college prior to her conversion. Through the years I have witnessed her life transformed like that of the Apostle Paul's. Evangelist Annette Gatlin is bold in her convictions and unashamed of the Gospel of Jesus Christ. Her life depicts total commitment, total trust and total surrender to God! *"Broken to be Repaired"* is truly a reflection of the spiritual journey traveled by my friend Evangelist Gatlin and a path of hope for others today.

Gwendolyn V. Jeffries
Retired Compensation Supervisor / City of Memphis

***

We are so excited and Godly proud of you.

Evangelist Annette Gatlin has a ministry to confront the deception and disillusion from the kingdom of darkness and we have been blessed to have known this mighty woman of God for over 15 years. God has given her revelation on the ministry of restoration and deliverance and the urgent need for it in the body of Christ. God has allowed Evangelist Gatlin through this book, "Broken to be Repaired" to be transparent exposing the enemy's devices used to try and stop the inner healing and deliverance she obtained. God has gifted her with knowing and recognizing his devices which is one of the most vital and important areas of ministry that cannot be overlooked.

This book, "Broken To Be Repaired" will lead you to the right path of God's divine plan for your life. You will learn how to recognize emotional scars, and why it is important for the body of Christ to minister to the emotional wounds of a person and nurture them through the process of healing. This book will help and encourage the reader to walk through every storm knowing God has a plan for their lives. They will learn to embrace the power of the Holy Spirit and with Him embrace every encounter and obstacle designed by God to help them break free.

Evangelist Gatlin knows firsthand how the power of God is revealed when a person is set free. For too long, the body of Christ has been blinded regarding the underlying issues that has kept them from having total deliverance. But today, God has risen in this powerful woman of God to expose ways in which God will repair you mentally, physically, emotionally and spiritually.

As you read the pages of this book you will be compelled to recognize the deception of the enemy and be set free and healed from your brokenness completely! Evangelist Gatlin's "life" and powerful testimony gives you the insights and tools of God's word for total restoration of your mind, body, and soul.

Senior Pastor- Sandra Thomas
Jacksonville Community Worship Center
Jacksonville, Arkansas 72076

***

This is a must read for anyone experiencing brokenness. I was instantly drawn in from the first chapter. Evangelist Gatlin establishes compassion and trust because, yes, she's been there too. It feels like having a talk with your favorite person who understands you. A therapeutic conversation where you can speak your truth without judgement, and feel HEARD. But your favorite person also holds you accountable to yourself. They love you too much to enable you to stay broken.

This book "Broken To Be Repaired" has captivating chapters like "Don't Bury Me Yet". Each page awaits you with a big hug filled with God's word and encouragement. This guide teaches you to speak life and command each day with daily affirmations and prayers. Your spirit will glow with peace beyond your own understanding.

Give yourself a chance to step out of the darkness, and back to a better YOU. Trust the process. Trust God. You will not regret reading this Christian therapy guide.

Monica Dillon

Broken To Be Repaired is an exceptional book. For anyone who is struggling to find their true self because of all the hurt and disappointments in life, this book is a must read!

Evangelist Annette Gatlin is a warrior of God. I had the pleasure of meeting her in 2012. She is a woman of Valor and allows her light to shine. Evangelist Gatlin has been through the fire and is sharing her heartfelt story with her readers on how they too can be victorious over their own challenges.

God has given her a powerful message to share her brokenness with her readers. Some say God, others say source, universe, or higher power; whatever your version this book encourages readers and gives them a sense of knowing they too will overcome. By opening your heart and connecting with God, your source, or the universe you are allowing God to heal and guide you in order for your purpose to be fulfilled.

Broken To Be Repaired inspires and gives hope to each reader. With everything going on in the world today, this book motivates readers to connect, step out on faith, and trust God knowing that each one of us has a higher calling. no matter what it looks like *all things work together for our good*. I highly recommend this book!

Thank you, Evangelist Annette Gatlin, for sharing your story allowing men and women around the world to be touched and healed.

Love and Blessings,
Tomika Hairston-Flood
Spiritual Life Transformation Coach
TRH UNIVERSAL VISION

***

I am reminded of what David stated in Psalm 34:19, "Many are the afflictions of the righteous, but the Lord delivers him out of them all." In her latest book, "Broken To Be Healed," Evangelist Annette Gatlin takes the reader through a detailed explanation of what it is to be broken and how the Lord will heal you as long as you are willing to go through the process.

So many times in life we experience loss, and because of the trials and tribulations of life, some of us fall into a place of despair. I believe Job said it best in Job 14:1, "Man that is born of a woman is of few days and full of trouble." However, the Words of Jesus resound clearly in John 16:33 when He decreed, "In the world ye shall have tribulation: but be of good cheer; I have overcome the world."

The Lord can use a person's afflictions, a person's brokenness to transform them into the empowering vessel HE created them to be. Evangelist Gatlin is a living testimony of that fact. Anyone that is currently experiencing a storm in their life will feel encouraged and empowered after reading and actively engaging in Evangelist Gatlin's insightful work. They will immediately realize that they are not just a conqueror, but MORE than a conqueror in Christ Jesus!

Rev. Tameka Lamb Green
Associate Minister and Elect Lady at Quinn Chapel A.M.E.
Church Crossett, AR

***

Trust in the Lord with all your heart and lean not to your own understanding.

In all thy ways acknowledge Him and he will direct your path. Proverbs 3:5-6

I have had the privilege of knowing Evangelist Annette Gatlin since 2005. God created a bond between us on the parking lot under a tree as we prayed for one another. I'm truly blessed and honored to have her as a friend and confidant. She is anointed and gifted by God. Her saying is always "Turn or Burn" as John the Baptist crying in the wilderness. She is a dynamic speaker, prayer warrior, mother, grandmother and friend. She has a heart of gold. God can truly heal anyone wherever they are hurting. To everyone that will read this book "Don't let your past keep you from getting to your future and all that God has for you.

One must always be obedient to the word of God and allow the Holy Spirit to lead and guide them. We must trust Him in every circumstance even when we don't understand why we must go through certain situations. Evangelist Annette Gatlin has truly been through some rough situations, but it was by the grace of God that she was not consumed, lost her mind or gave up completely.

The information she shared will touch the lives of many people who have dealt with low self-esteem, disappointments, hurt, pain, and rejection. Some people would have lost their faith & hope that things would not get better, but GOD! We must remember that even when the road gets tough to never give up or quit. Reading this book will transform lives and the way people think. We all will be able to be healed, delivered, set free and experience the life that God wants us to have. People will think if she was able to persevere, then so can we.

Elder Carol Collins-Associate Minister
Intercessor and Prayer Counselor
Nurse Practitioner at VA Medical Center

***

As you read through the pages of *"Broken To Be Repaired"*, it reminds us of how through life we are pressed against struggle, fight against adversities, conquer fears and are restored after losses. This rendition of the collaboration of faith, prayer, and dedication to The Lord is a work of love. It also reflects the courage to go on, encourage others, and yourself to remain with Jesus through it all and through The Word of God. Evangelist Annette Gatlin, Women of God with a mantle of winning souls for Jesus Christ at all cost.

Prophetess Minister Lori Allen

***

"Broken to Be Repaired" is a must read! It's "The standard" spoken from the heart of God! Evangelist Gatlin, for as long as I have known her, has

always had a yearning to motivate others to stand firmly on the word of God. She is a powerhouse, takes charge, and a woman of unshakable faith! Her transparency is a window view of frontline battles and victories. We have defeated him (the adversary) by the Blood of the Lamb and the power of our testimony!

Call her with a mountain of troubles and before you breathe twice she is bombarding Heaven on your behalf. Gatlin is a warrior equipped with a barrage of prayer for any situation. She is on assignment! She is well studied and approved! Give her your brokenness, and she'll give you unadulterated Jesus! Evangelist Gatlin is a beautiful anointed vessel filled with ministry.

This is a pure guide for healing and righteous direction. The "WoW" factor of *Broken to Be Repaired* is how eloquently Evangelist Gatlin ushers your spirit into a crescendo of high praise. By the time you reach the affirmations your heart will race with boldness of praise that seeps up from the depths of your belly (your soul cry!) You will begin to read out loud with conviction the promises of God that will feed and fortify your soul!

Lady Kim Mondersir Johnson

***

I have known Evangelist Gatlin for a number of years. She is a "God fearing, Christian woman, who always "seeks the Lord's advice" and guidance from His word before making any decision for herself or her family.

God has brought Evangelist Gatlin a long way on her journey of self-discovery, acceptance and purpose. With the grace of God, continuous prayer and faithfulness in His word, she has opened her heart to the Lord and to you, the readers, with honesty and truthfulness.

She "cried out to the Almighty" and found her purpose, "to help others repair their brokenness with the grace of God"! And you can, too. Once a "broken vessel", she's now a "fulfilled purposeful woman after God's own heart"!

Allow God to help you "pick up your broken pieces" just as He did for Evangelist Gatlin and "be repaired"! "Grace and peace to you from God our Father and the Lord Jesus Christ, who gave Himself to rescue us from the present evil age, according to the will of our God and Father, to whom be glory forever and ever.

Amen."
Galatians 3-5

Love, peace and continued blessing,
Ella Revely
Church Steward Board Member

Broken to be Repaired is a book written for the ages! It is a book that encourages all of God's people to stand strong in his word and in his love. Reading this book gives you the inner strength you need to love yourself as strongly as God does. While reading this, I felt the hand of God on my shoulder as I was guided by the words of an anointed Woman of God. A great book that teaches life long lessons that we wished we had known years ago.

Anjalah Hughes Grant
Heart Team

***

"Life-changing…a perfect prescription for total healing and an open door to rediscovering who you are, your purpose in life and God's plan for your life. Enjoy your new journey."

Pastor Terrosa Buie
Journey to Life International
pastort@journeytolifeinternational.org

***

I had the opportunity 23 years ago to meet this powerful woman of God, Evangelist Annette Hines Gatlin.

Setting the stage;

As I was standing in line at Marshalls department store, I heard from behind what sounded like a roaring lion, fiercely and boldly declaring the Word of God.

I turned around to see where the thunderous voice was coming from, I began to listen carefully and was amazed and captivated by the conversation she was having, as we were all waiting to layaway items.

Little did I know that this moment was divinely orchestrated.

I am Prophetess Diane Herron. I was called at an early age by Jesus Christ Himself. Called to the Ministry of Intercession, I am in Love with Him. Having dealt with issues of rejection, low self-esteem, mistreated, abused, fear and illnesses, brought me to a place where wrong and bad choices made me a candidate for *"Broken To Be Repaired."*

I have worked and been trained by many teachers as well as life's circumstances. Evangelist Gatlin and I became friends as well as co-laborers in the Ministry. Our lives were parallel in many ways. We were both Chosen, Anointed, and Appointed.

Again, in remembering the layaway department, little did we know the meaning of putting away seed in the ground with the expectation of a harvest. When you put a seed in the ground the process changes the composition. Botanically we know once sown, it germinates. A seed consists of a protected seed covering, some kind of storage tissue with nutrient reserves, and a dormant embryo. We further know that under the correct conditions the dormant embryo can be awakened to germinate and grow into a mature plant. *"Broken to Be Repaired"* Is synonymous with seed germination.

Jesus said in John 12:24-25, Very truly I tell you, unless a grain of wheat falls into the earth and dies, it remains just a single grain, but if it dies it yields much fruit.

As you venture on this Powerful journey of Worship, this book will help you to understand the overwhelming love and grace of God that compelled him to place the very Lamb of God into the body of a teenage girl, to be born into a culture that would hound him at every turn to be nailed to the nightmare of our sinful lives.

I praise God for this vessel sharing with us her journey to wholeness. I have watched her live out the very words in which she has written allowing herself to become transparent and used for the Glory of God. I have watched her grow into a beautiful mature plant, more than capable of empowering the people of God with much discipline.

Thank you, Evangelist, for sharing with the world your transformation, May God continue to use you, May He Anoint you even more for His service. I am truly honored to be a part of your life and I love you In the Lord.

In His Service,
Prophetess Diane Herron

***

Evangelist Annette Gatlin's book Broken to be Repaired" is an eye opening book for those who wish to allow themselves to heal from broken dreams, promises and more. Her testimony and transparency allow anyone to know they can be healed from anything that has been broken in their life. Truly this book will be a blessing to all who read it.

Rev. Regina Clay
Author
ReginaClay.com

***

Broken to be Repaired is a must-read for anyone who has found themselves contemplating what to do with the pieces of their life that remain. If you are dealing with low self-esteem, insecurities, rejection, addiction or just looking for purpose this guide is for you.

Read this book and allow Evangelist Annette Gatlin to mentor and lead you to healing and transformation. Welcome to purpose!

Elder La Quandria Johnson
CEO of KEY Consulting: Knowledge Empowers You
Facebook La Quandria Johnson

***

"BROKEN TO BE REPAIRED"

This book by Evangelist Gatlin conveys to the reader the definition of broken by God and how that He is seen by the reader through life's difficulties and journey. She not only explains how being broken by God affects the reader, but she also identifies how the reader grows in faith and trust in God.

Being weak, a definition the world designates to anyone who trusts in God and walks with God and answers to God for their everyday solutions and behaviors is strength to the Christian, followers of Christ, who study the Word of God. This book highlights many solutions from daily affirmations, reading the Word of God, and accepting Christ as their personal Savior.

Evangelist Gatlin closes each chapter with a prayer that solidifies the information gleaned by the reader. She offers her personal testimony to advise the reader they need not come to Christ perfect but as they are, He will accept them. She offers scriptures and Bible Heroes to give credence to her words of faith and encouragement. A must read for the new babe in Christ and to the seasoned Christian who has walked years with Christ.

Evangelist Deborah Adisa
ACTS Ministries, North Little Rock, Arkansas, Suffragen Bishop

Pastor Frank Stewart
Deborah Adisa, RN, Staff Nurse, Conway Behavioral
Health Hospital, Conway, Arkansas 72034

We are so excited and Godly proud of you Evangelist Gatlin.

Now, more than any other time in our modern history, the human has become more acutely aware of what the world calls "imperfections". God calls them "human characteristics. We need Him now, to help us discover the strengths in our perceived weaknesses.

This is an awesome book!

God has His hand on this process throughout and all your "life" experiences have you to the eye-opening revelations. We bear witness to the hand of God being on you by His gift that is in you to teach others to begin the process of healing. The "breaking" and allowing God to repair is truly the key to building Godly character.

God will help us to work through the frustration, anger and disappointments of life. "For HE knows" the plan and course set for our lives. He knows the plans that are meant to build character and not to cuddle or shelter us.

Thank you for stating it so plainly in this book, "Broken To Be Repaired."

May our FATHER in Heaven continue to inform and inspire you to higher heights and deeper depths as you continue His mission. May God continue to richly bless you Evangelist Gatlin with revelation, in Jesus' name, Amen.

Overseer W. T. Thomas
Jacksonville Community Worship Center
Jacksonville, Arkansas

BROKEN
TO BE
Repaired

A GUIDE FOR HEALING YOUR
MIND, BODY, AND SOUL

ANNETTE GATLIN

authorHOUSE®

AuthorHouse™
1663 Liberty Drive
Bloomington, IN 47403
www.authorhouse.com
Phone: 833-262-8899

Published by AuthorHouse 11/20/2020

ISBN: 978-1-6655-0739-4 (sc)
ISBN: 978-1-6655-0738-7 (e)

Library of Congress Control Number: 2020922260

Print information available on the last page.

Cover designed by Claire Lesesne, owner of J&C Designs

This book is printed on acid-free paper.

Scriptures were taken from the King James Version of the Bible.

TRIBUTE

In loving memory of my beloved Mother and Father: Mary Elizabeth Hines (03/22/1940-09/04/2004), and James Eddie Hines (02/01/1936-02/14/2011).

May the peace of God continue to be with my family forever and always.

CONTENTS

FOREWORD

Broken to be Repaired by Evangelist Annette Hines-Gatlin, is written from an experiential and biblical perspective on the values of allowing the Lord to heal and restore you in your broken place. Within these pages she shares her own journey and experience of being in the lowest state, not ever thinking that she could be repaired or heal from her own painful wounds and hurt.

Every person at some point in his or her life experiences being in a broken state. Being in a broken state feels like your life is fragmented in 1000 pieces like a puzzle and you can't figure out how to put it back together again. It is in that state when we cry out to God and get to the place of total surrender for God, to begin to put us back together and to repair those broken places. These broken places are caused by our childhood trauma of molestation or rape, sickness, experiencing rejection and abandonment, grief, loneliness, betrayal, depression, and divorce. When all the smoke is settled we find that we have the victory through Christ Jesus. Where the enemy sees our defeat, God sees our victory! It is then when, Yeshua HaMashiach, "The Anointed One", our savior delivers us.

Evangelist Annette Hines-Gatlin pours out of her very own experience of being broken only to be repaired. The heartbeat and summation of this entire book as Evangelist Gatlin so eloquently puts it and I quote, "When we comprehend and clear our heads after the breaking, the ashes and residue becomes beautiful."

In this book, you will find prayers for reflection and daily affirmations that will boost your spirit man and encourage you throughout the day, to keep moving forward from Broken to being Repaired. Brokenness is a part of everyone's life, but that does not mean that you are too broken to not be repaired by God's loving grace, mercy, and kindness.

You will find yourself somewhere in this book, *Broken to be Repaired*. I believe by the time you finish reading this, you will find your new power, resilience, restoration, purpose, and destiny. You will gain a new strength to navigate through your challenges and allow God's healing power in your broken place.

It gives me great pleasure and honor to write the foreword for this book, because at one point I too was Broken in need of Repair. I was a fragmented being. I know all too well about being wounded, and experiencing the pain, and hurt caused by childhood trauma, divorce, rejection, grief, betrayal, and lies. It wasn't until I accepted and received my deliverance, that I was able to see the beauty out of the ashes and residue of my fiery trials.

This book is an excellent motivational and inspirational tool for anyone that wants to know just how they can recover. Yes, it's easier said than done, but once it is done and you're repaired, it becomes easier.

Congratulations, WOG

Dr. Tamika Wilson
Dr. Tamika Ministries LLC
DTM School of Advanced Biblical Studies, Provost
Philadelphia, PA
Author of: *Hermeneutics, Equipping God's People with the Keys to Unlock God's Word* and *The Gift of Prophecy, Raising Samuels "A Guide for Emerging Prophets"*

ACKNOWLEDGEMENTS

First and foremost, I give all praises to God, the Creator of all things. I am truly thankful for the wisdom and insights that He has given me in regards to the "breaking" process, as it has been designed to develop my character. God uses our life's experiences to fulfill His purpose in us and through us by His Holy Spirit. Most of all I thank Him for allowing me to be an example of a "work-in-progress". While I continue to learn how to depend solely on Him and His infinite Word, I give all the glory and honor to His majestic name! Jesus truly remains the center of my joy and my strength.

Although I have many standing with me and undergirding me with spiritual counsel, I would like to recognize and thank the following people who nurtured, loved, and encouraged me to continue my walk with God:

My beloved husband, the late Bishop Charles Edward Gatlin, for his love and support. His astounding fatherly affection to our children will always be cherished. (5/8/1951-2/28/2013).

My children: Lydia Smith, Shandra Benson, Rodney Dillon Jr., and Kelsey Dillon. Thank you for understanding that my strict discipline was not aimed to hurt you but to guide you in the best way possible. When you were born, I fell ignorant to the knowledge of the correct way to raise children. I had no idea which was the right or the wrong way in helping to lead and direct you. However, as I submitted my motherly instincts to God, He taught me how to raise you in the admiration of Him. I pray that you teach your children the ways of the Lord and help guide them to their destiny. I am very proud to be your Mom, and I enjoy watching you evolve. I love you.

Brother and Sisters: Larry D. Hines, Mary C. Hines, Janie M. Jackson (Otis), Paula Hines, and Priscilla Doston (Minda). Thank you for being a significant part of my life and encouraging me to push harder in pursuing my purpose. Your consistent love and support is acknowledged and greatly appreciated.

Grandchildren (Nana's babies): Terrell Smith, Kennedy Smith, Iden Smith, Aamira Smith, Christian Bonner Jr, and Cai Bonner. May you continue to pursue your dreams, as I am here to help you mature and fulfill your purpose on earth. I love you, Nana.

Claire Lesesne Founder and CEO of J&C Designs: A special thanks to my awesome graphic designer and book cover creator. Your expertise in grasping my thoughts and expressing them in print is extraordinary and with great admiration! Thank You.

Spiritual Parents: Bishop Walter L. Branch and Evangelist Mary Branch for teaching biblical truths as the Holy Spirit led them and the true beauty of Holiness. Your encouragement and prayers have helped me to blossom through many cumbersome channels of opposition, whereas I have become triumphant through travail.

Zsilas Micheal Hughes: To say the least, you are a man of great wisdom with the insights to help catapult a dreamer's dream. Your millennium gift of leadership and mentorship, along with your generosity in helping to bring this project into full fruition is impeccable! I am eternally grateful.

With such warm admiration and love for my mother and her children, I am eternally grateful for the unswerving friendship of

Mr. Cecil and Mrs. Joyce Sellers, Tom and Kara Preston, Rob and Suzanne Preston, and the Bell's family.

For your continued prayers and continued friendship through it all, I would like to pay homage to Chad and Elder Francine Lewis, Dr. Levenis Penix, Pastor Kathy Halfacre, Apostle Jacqueline Smith, Terrance and Pastor Sheila Britt, Evangelist-Missionary Darlene McCoy, Dr. Dorothy Daniels, Bishop U. S. and Bishop Marylin Reed, Rodney and Sandra Sample, Earnest & Evangelist Sandra Burnett, and Sherrolyn Newell for the guidance and impartations through my walk of faith. They encouraged me to always speak whatever God bestows upon my tongue and to stay focused while moving toward the things of God. They have been by my side for many years in which I am eternally grateful for continued prayer and also a genuine friendship.

Whether we have connected through mere passing or years of comradery, may all of you be enlightened by God's intimate love as you read this book.

To God be all the Glory.

INTRODUCTION

What do you want out of life? As you travel through this journey called life, may this book guide, enhance, motivate, and encourage you, as you allow God to direct your path. "*Broken To Be Repaired*", A Guide For Healing Your Mind, Body, and Soul is specifically designed and written to serve as a plan of action, for restoration and recovery. This book provides instructions, explaining how one can be broken in order to be healed. You may become broken, fragmented, detached, and feel a sense of false hope during trials and while coping with issues of life. In order to exit out of your cycle of brokenness, you must PREPARE TO BE REPAIRED! The process of repairing a broken place is one that allows opportunities for obedience, growth, maturity, and healing while you overcome your insecurities and find God's peace and clarity. Your healing has begun, receive it now.

God expects us to strive for spiritual maturity as we travel on this journey of faith and celebrate victory over defeat. "Broken to be Repaired" will open your understanding of how God can reconstruct your life. It is emphasized throughout the book that God is in control and is willing to restore the brokenness if given the opportunity to reshape your life. What can be more exciting than being totally repaired after a great disappointment or a long term illness? I am excited to venture this journey alongside you in being restored from past wounds, hurt, and pain. Now let the healing begin. As you delve in you will discover things that you've allowed to lay domat, regain confidence, get your fight back, draw closer to the Lord, and experience God's love and His unmerited favor for your life. "Healing is the Children's Bread." Let your journey begin.

CHAPTER ONE

PERSONAL ANECDOTE

ME

"Never underestimate the power of dreams and the influence of the human Spirit. We are all the same in this notion; the potential for greatness lies within each of us." (Wilma Rudolph)

Are you aware of your strengths?

Have you acknowledged any of your weaknesses?

Can you even imagine yourself being broken as a clay pot?

Are you broken?

My ultimate question is: "Do you really know who you are and who you are called to be?" Take a long look at yourself in the mirror. What do you see? Who's looking back at you? Do you want to know who that person really is? If you are unable to firmly answer these questions with intent, I admonish you to proceed reading. As you continue to analyze your situation, you will be able to answer these complex questions with simple answers. If you will allow me to help you discover your true identity, your journey will consist of restoration, healing, and the increase of the presence of God.

At one time, these were all questions I asked myself. The person I saw was an illusion, just a figment of my imagination. This person was someone who lacked the internal flame to prosper, not only as a human being, but as a purposed-woman of God. I wanted to be real with myself. I desired to be a person of substance and integrity in all aspects of my life. Going through the motions lifelessly, I came to a realization that I was fabricating my own happiness and it was all a persona. When I recognized that all of my insecurities came out in my private moments, reality established itself. I was hiding behind the mask to keep people out.

The mask that many of us put on to hide our realities from others and also in efforts to hide the reality of what we are actually experiencing from ourselves. Even after my educational achievements of graduating with honors and obtaining three college degrees, I still felt incomplete, unsatisfied, and depleted of any sense of success. I was incapable of being my personal cheerleader or appreciating my own accomplishments. My past pain immobilized my ability to believe in myself and not to mention my dreams. Everything that surrounded me, I believed was working against me, maybe just as aggressive or less passive in its intensity.

Have you ever found yourself at this point? Have you been in a place where you accepted the worst in everything and denied all possibilities of a positive outcome? It is at this place where you must realize that you are *broken* and need to be *repaired*. This book is intended to bring you into awareness that without God, you are a broken vessel whose potential is limited. To say the least, divine healing is a significant process in God's strategic plan that is required when establishing your purpose.

As a woman in pursuit of happiness, I have navigated through the world infatuated by others' perception of who I am and what I would become. As people who approach life with a humbling mindset, we often authorize those whom we perceive as superior to prophesy inaccurate and inadequate visions of who we really are. As of this moment, those negative predictions end here. Not only for me, but you too can be repaired, restored, and refreshed. Yes! You can be healed and set free from the fear of your past rejection, and not being motivated to maximize your potential.

In this personal antidote, before we can proceed I need you to recognize that of which God acknowledges. He only acknowledges what He created. And because you were created in His image, you must realize that when He looks at you, He sees an image of Himself. As a matter of fact, He saw you before your father ever thought about planting the seed. He knew you before your mother knew that the seed had been planted. So since He preplanned your existence, no matter how you arrived, not only must you learn to see what He sees. You must learn to feel how He feels about you, as well as speak what He says about you.

How soon you receive God's healing will be determined by your faith in His plan and purpose for your life. According to Jeremiah 29:11 it reads, ***"I know the thoughts that I think toward you, saith the Lord, thoughts of peace, and not of evil, to give you an expected end."*** Jeremiah assured Judah that after their exile in Babylon, that God would bring them into the promised land. However, in this declaration we must be willing participants! One must align with the will of God for your life's destiny to unfold. With that in mind, let's begin by giving God permission to pick up the pieces of your brokenness. At this point, I can venture into the journey with you. Be courageous and be bold as you follow the Lord's guidance. As a woman of God, I am a vessel that is used to bring forth this message in order for you to inhabit the presence of God, where lies the fullness of joy for your potential growth. In order to exit out of your cycle of brokenness, you must PREPARE TO BE REPAIRED! This is your **EXODUS** moment! It is in this initial phase that you must be willing to submit your understanding, confidence, and actions to the plan of God in order to receive the information.

Personally, I have struggled with low self-esteem, physical and chronic illnesses, and rejection. From a young age, it was always difficult to see myself as a beautiful person. The multitude of unexplainable blemishes that presented on my face caused internal insecurities. These internal insecurities created a similar effect externally. This is because the root of our inner being is reflected and projected in our outward daily appearance. Looking in the mirror, I couldn't see my potential for growth because I focused on the flaws. Have you ever heard the comical saying as Anthelme Brillat-Savarin said in 1826; *"You are what you eat."* (Hyman, P. (2015). This is similar in the same aspect. You are what you consume. You can consume information, energy, and influence not only physically, but both mentally and emotionally. If you consume negativity, it will manifest externally, the same rule applies with positivity. Because of the exterior flaws, it was hard to get past the internal emptiness that God wanted to fill with observable qualities. Notice the importance of the relationship between both internal and external. If I am speaking to you, continue reading, and let's walk it out.

Unfortunately, I was totally oblivious to God's purpose in my creation. Prior to my personal repair, I lacked the mental acknowledgement of God. The bible tells us that we must always move in a manner that is reflective of God and his ways. "***In all thy ways acknowledge him, and he shall direct your paths***." (Prov. 3:6). As a consequence, I suffered many physical-chronic discomforts for many years. After being diagnosed at an early age with a degenerative bone disease, massive nerve-damage, and stenosis of the spine, I found myself unable to keep my balance. I've had many horrible falls and several surgeries to help aid my body's performance. The pains are horrific! The emotional struggle is a reflection of the physical pain. From a walker to a cane, additional support was necessary in order to keep me standing. Doctors could not ensure the absence of future falls. All of which was not as painful as the rejection and mocking! The scars hidden to the physical eye continued to instill internal wounds. This enabled me to hold my own stance through my faith in his healing virtue. My physical disabilities made me a candidate for healing. Never look at your disability as an impossibility, see it as a challenge for your betterment. In Mark 9:23 Jesus said unto him, "***If thou canst believe, all things are possible to him that believeth.***" You must believe in order for transformation to take place. I was not able to receive the manifestation of His healing power until I allowed my faith **in** Him to open up **and let** Him in. Ultimately, I had to evolve into a space where I could speak to my situation and command it to align with the will of God. Now I realize that my faith, obedience, and trust in God's Word is sufficient enough for Him to move on my behalf. Gratefully, in return I was broken and repaired over a period of time and I continue to heal, grow, and prosper. You have to understand that you will progressively heal as you take one step at a time. The process of repairing a broken place is one that allows opportunities for obedience, growth, maturity, and healing. Aimlessly, your transformation will manifest through your faith in God's breaking and restoration process.

"Though He were a Son, yet he learned obedience by the things which He suffered; And being made perfect, He became the author of eternal salvation unto all them that obey Him; Called of God an high priest after the order of Melchisedec." (Heb. 5:8-10).

After all, were you not created to imitate Jesus? Yes, He had to go through the process of being broken and repaired by the Father. Needless to say, God gave Him the strength to endure, as He will you. Of course, life will have its challenges, but if you take advantage of this journey of being broken to be repaired, you will overcome your insecurities and find God's peace and clarity. Even if the physical body does not receive total healing, you must believe that God is able to help you endure the process through faith.

This book invites the reader into a channel of twists and turns, seeing how one can truly be broken in order to be healed. It will encourage you to walk with God and be healed by his Holy Spirit. You will learn to go the extra mile, even through the storms of life that you will encounter. Most of all you will learn that you will recover after each obstacle, one at a time. It is designed to help you take responsibility for limitations you built and destroy those limitations. God wants to remove the feeling of conformity and "inside the box" thinking, and help you break free. Most of all this book will help you expand outside the box and reach your full potential.

I must emphasize my point further that with God we are vessels whose capability and potential is without limit.

My whole purpose in writing this book is to help you take a closer look at the things that caused you to stop believing in the Lord's plan for your life. The process is intentional and purposeful. It is to help you gain your confidence in God. It is to eliminate the fear of failure and break free from wrong perceptions of yourself and your journey. You will learn to accept His healing to be restored and repaired Mentally, Physically, Emotionally, and Spiritually.

As we become willing to suffer challenges and adversities, we are then molded into His image and are able to receive his unconditional love. His love is by far the greatest benefit that we could ever receive. We are able to be blessed when we are humble enough to complete His work within ourselves by daily practice. The process of being broken to be repaired, is just what God revealed to me. Which simply means, ***"Broken to be Repaired."*** The pain, hurt, and wounds are all part of the process.

Despite your flaws and imperfections, healing awaits you if you can only believe that God has a plan and purpose for your life. If you believe what you have read this far, your healing has already begun. While the Spirit has begun the process of change, begin to take this journey in stride and enjoy your victory over your insecurities and imperfections. As His strength is made perfect in your weakness, promotion and transformation are inevitable.

Promotion and transformation will propel you in the right path for God's divine direction for both you, and the lives of your children, as well as the generations to come. As many people are suffering in silence in this season, it is time for the cycle of brokenness to be repaired. As you yield and align your will to the will of God, your silence of inner pain will start to heal.

The mother eagle does not discharge her eaglets from the nest in efforts to harm them. Rather, she makes it unbearable through the depletion of provided sustenance so that they will learn to to support themselves. These eaglets learn to gather their own food, travel safely, and return back to the nest slowly until it is time for them to build their own nest. Otherwise, they will be like the chicken that is pinned down to the ground that never learns its true potential. For an eaglet to learn to soar above the storm, the mother has to teach it to stand on its own. Only during the survival process will the eagle get its wings and learn to fly high. That is similar to what God does with us. By making it uncomfortable and teaching us His way, we learn how to trust His will. Just as the eagle acknowledges his lineage in the storm, we must acknowledge the LORD of our lives.

So let the winds blow, let the rain fall, and let the journey begin. Allow the storms of life to mount you up for your destiny. Recognize this as a humbling experience that will mature you both spiritually and emotionally. And no matter what obstacles are placed in front of you during your process of being broken, accept what God allows, and do NOT give up. He has promised to be with you, even in the most difficult times. For the greater change within you, remember that you are called to complete some tasks that only you can fulfill.

- Side note: The name, satan, will not be capitalized in this book because I do not acknowledge him as having any power in our lives.

INSERT 1-3 BROKEN PLACES THAT YOU HAVE STRUGGLED WITH THAT YOU ARE NOW BELIEVING GOD TO REPAIR:

_____

_____

_____

PERSONAL EXAMPLES OF MY OWN REPAIRS:

1. *Low self-esteem because of what others would say about my spots on my face and skin. Insecurities of not knowing who I was created to be and what God's purpose was for my life.*
2. *Physical-chronic illnesses, diagnosed with degenerative bone disease and stenosis of the spine. I suffered for many years trusting that God would either heal me from it or help me to endure the pain because of my faith in His Word.*
3. *Rejection, divorce, drugs, alcohol, probation, and rape. The Shame and guilt of failing over and over again.*
4. *An abusive marriage.*
5. *Trusting God to provide through the struggle of going from welfare to entrepreneurship in a successful Cosmetology business. Which all took faith in God's word. I am now retired and completely dependent on God's provision in the replacement of my capabilities.*

Prayer:

Father God, in the name of Jesus, we give thanks and honor to You. For You are worthy to be praised! Lord help us to submit to Your will and plans that You have for our lives. We thank You for humbling us, so that we can be used for the building of the Kingdom of God. Even in our brokenness, we ask that You transform us into the perfect image of Christ. Allow our lives to be an illuminated light that will draw others back to You by the blood of the Lamb and the words of our testimony. Lord, help us to trust and depend on You through the most difficult times that are ahead. Remind us that if we turn away from Your ways, our lives will have no peace. It is in Christ alone that we find peace. Repair us now for the Master's use. And allow the "breaking" to prepare us to accept our divine healing during the difficult times. In Jesus Name,

Amen

CHAPTER TWO

GOD RESTORES WHAT REMAINS

TRANSFORMATION TAKES PLACE IN BROKENNESS

What does it mean to be broken?

What justifies the classification of brokenness?

Being broken has such a negative meaning, because when we hear that something is broken, we are programmed to think the worst. We see broken as something that was once whole but is now shattered in multiple pieces.

In this context, brokenness can be seen as a person or an object. For instance, let's take a glass plate, or a simple, white dinner plate. What if you are setting the table for dinner and you happen to drop the plate on the floor and it shattered into pieces? If you are home with family members, they would likely come and inquire as to what the commotion was caused by. "What's happened?" they might ask. Perhaps, you would emotionally respond with: "It's broken! I broke a dinner plate."

A child in this position would almost certainly feel fearful of how his/her parents would respond. On the other hand, an adult might feel frustrated or angry, or concerned that a dinner set is incomplete. Personally, what we fear of being broken or incomplete is how others might judge us or respond to our worthlessness or insignificance. Certainly, your feelings are not unjustified; however, they are valid as to the purpose that God has in your brokenness. The true meaning of broken is to be fractured, damaged, and/or no longer in one piece. Not being in God's "working order," maybe the problem is that you are intuitively feeling that your purpose is being compromised.

Alternatively, God sees you as a *broken vessel to be repaired*. And while He is eager to **restore what remains and transform your broken pieces into containers of miracles and blessings,** here is how Romans 5:3-5 defends God's plan for you it says, *"And not only so, but we glory in tribulations also: knowing that tribulation worketh patience; And patience, experience; and experience, hope: And hope maketh not ashamed; because* *the love of God is shed abroad in our hearts by the Holy Ghost which is given unto us."* (Rom. 5:3-5). Amen.

In other words, God wants to show up **for** you so that those **around** you can see His transformation **in** you. He is waiting to take your brokenness and not only make you whole, but make you brand new again. To put it simply, the Lord will sever what is painful, abusive, and what is considered waste in your life, only to renew the right spirit within you. God wants to use your broken pieces to become His **MASTERPIECE!** That's how deep **His love** is for **us**. Who wouldn't want to become a vessel for the Master's use? I know that you want the **best** for your life and this journey of testing to be **rewarding**! When you become aware that God is willing to take your broken pieces and put them on display for His own glory, it gives you a deeper revelation and a stronger appreciation for what it means to be clay in the Potter's hand. Becoming a vessel is when you allow God to be the director of you and your life, giving him permission to use you in ways that are pleasing to Him. This means that you have a responsibility to showcase your God given gifts and talents to his people both lost and found. In showcasing your talents, you are responsible for displaying what is possible through God. You are able to create, perform, and excel in ways that are unable to be explained.

"Then I went down to the Potter's house, and, behold, He wrought a work on the wheels. And the vessel that He made of clay was marred in the hand of the Potter: so He made it again another vessel, as seemed good to the Potter to make it" (Jer. 18:3-4). God is able to make anything new and whole, but it is up to us to participate in the process. Oftentimes, other people identify and place judgment on the defects of those around them, all whereas inhabiting the same or similar traits of those being judged. Even as they are staring at their own reflection,

whether in a mirror, a passing window, or a glimpse of their own silhouette, we must not allow them to condemn what we refuse to acknowledge about ourselves. Know your worth and accept nothing less of what God has placed on your name. Acknowledge that you are a purposed child of God who is blessed and highly favored.

By participating with the Potter, we must face the reality of what our past flaws, imperfections, and wounds have created. What we must be willing to do with those scars that remind us of our previous pain that impacts our future observation of self, is to become, again, a vessel. We have to hand over our life to the father so that he may use our flaws for the benefit of his people through showing what is possible in Christ. Indeed, pain, more often than not, impacts the mental, physical, emotional, and spiritual awareness that is imperative when searching for internal affirmation. However, when you are able to come into personal agreement that you have been "***Broken to be Repaired***," *transformation can take place in brokenness.*

Whether the afflictions were a failed marriage, drug addiction, loss of a loved-one, paranoid about your appearance, financial stress, domestic violence, or even rape, **GOD RESTORES WHAT REMAINS!** These all are set-ups for come-backs! So TRUST THE **PLAN OF GOD** AND NOT THE **PAIN.** God has a funny way of allowing us to tread down a path that is not conducive to our vision in terms of finance, mental and emotional wellness, or just mere maturity. Many times He wants to use our pain to become our pulpit. Just learn to relax and go with the flow! Understand that when God is testing our faith, we will encounter challenges that test our ability to be persistent in trusting the work of the Lord. You must be strong enough to withstand the hardships of life and put your trust in Him. This will result in a blessing from the Lord that you won't have enough room to receive.

For years, I tried to hide behind my makeup. Why? Because I felt comfort in knowing that my blemishes were being hidden from those whom I felt would criticize me. Because I felt more comfortable around people when my blemishes were covered, I thought that the full-coverage foundation is what gave me the ability to be outspoken and live boldly. Anyone who took a first glance almost always had a shocking reaction.

Not only were questions asked that embedded a sense of humiliation, and decreased my confidence, there were questions asked that made me inquire "Is there something really wrong with me?" They gave me an internal acceptance that I was considered anything less than beautiful and humble. Questions that people asked both out of curiosity and with enthusiasm would include questions like: "What happened to your face?" Or, "What's wrong with your skin?", " Why do you have all of those spots?" There was even the daily commentary that total strangers voiced like: "Wow! That's UGLY! Is it contagious?" Even so, hiding the imperfections on my face gave me the empowerment that I needed to gain confidence.

Consistently, people are programmed to instinctively cover their wounds, pain, or hurts with a smile. Whereas makeup can be used as a similar tool, it dismisses the lingering thought that our scars are visible. Makeup may cover the marks from the natural eye, but it does not prevent negative words from imparting fears and anxieties. Such fear creates hindrance in our ability to comprehend who we really are in God. Think about it. Even if you are the cause of your own wound, pain, or hurt, the first step in the process of healing and transformation is to forgive YOURSELF. It's never too late to get it right.

Transformation begins in the heart (mind) of man. In order to realize your potential for greatness and acknowledge your identity in God, you must first examine what unidentified you with His purpose in your life. Life happens! And whatever has happened was no surprise to God. He already knew you before He actually created you. Becoming aware of this reality and operating in this mentality will create a sense of self-worth like you have never known. Otherwise, negative self-esteem prevents the opportunity to engage in self-admiration.

Through generous blessings, we have been granted gifts and talents that were intended to be used to glorify God, while making others aware of His wonderful creation. You must keep in mind that the beauty in which the Universe was created, is the same beauty that is infused in you. You are created in the image and likeness of God. That makes you His most precious creation. Take a moment and think about all that God has created. All the beauty that lies in the world was all premeditated. From every grain of grass that lay under your feet to every bird that flies above your head in the sky, God created so that we may enjoy. In Genesis 1:26-27 it reads, "***And God said, Let us make man in our image, after our likeness: and let them have dominion over the fish of the sea, and over the fowl of the air, and over the cattle, and over all the earth, and over every creeping thing that creepeth upon the earth. So God created man in his own image, in the image of God created he him; male and female created he them.***" God had a perfect time in which He created everything.

What Ecclesiastes 3:11 says about God's timing is this: ***"He hath made every thing beautiful in his time: also he hath set the world in their heart, so that no man can find out the work that God maketh from the beginning to the end."***

Whereas the course many of us take lands us in the wrong

direction, life happens to us all and we choose wrong directions. I know that I am guilty of taking **U-TURNS, DETOURS,** and **DELAYS**! Operating from a place of hurt and pain, we too often allow our emotions to get the best of us. Even if unnecessary affliction is the cause of your spiritual demise, it's time to awake from your stumble and realize that **GOD RESTORES WHAT REMAINS**! If you want a different outcome, you need to make a move and allow the transformation to take place in your brokenness. In getting a different outcome take the route that God leads you. He said; *"And thine ears shall hear a word behind thee, saying, This is the way, walk ye in it, when ye turn to the right hand, and when ye turn to the left."* (Isa. 30:21). You have been *"Broken to be Repaired!"* God wants us to listen to his voice only.

Distraction hinders our development. To say the least, unhealthy attachments and a limited mentality can distract you from evolving in a way that is conducive to the process. And that's not only in life, but the life that Christ intends for you to live. Stop allowing mental blocks to delay your progress, such obstructions as failed relationships, financial ruin, divorce, miscarriage, or particularly abortion. Envision the vision that God has for you, while He patiently awaits for your eyes to become open. Detour if you must, and know that God is there to direct your path. Now trust His lead because destiny is calling **your** name!

The Lord says in Habakkuk 2:2 *"And the Lord answered me, and said, Write the vision, and make it plain upon tables, that he may run that readeth it."* **See, you must write out your vision so clear that others become ecstatic about it!**

Once your vision is observed, not only will they be encouraged to run with it, they will rush to accomplish the task at hand. Life has a way of releasing the truth about our "**crutches**." These are distractions that keep us fragile and bound to our insecurities.

Refusing to address our frailties merely reopens the wound. Left open to continue bleeding onto others, it becomes a constant reminder of who or what caused the pain.

You have to choose to let go of the past hurts and forgive whoever or whatever caused the (**pain**) breach. In doing so, God's healing process can be implicated through you as you devour the very core and root of bitterness. Moreover, any infectious residue that remains can be severed away and purged from the inner man. When your attention is turned towards the truth of who God says you are, ***God will restore what remains****, and* you will encounter new possibilities for CHANGE!

While I can assume that you desire a better surrounding, a better outlook and perspective on life, my question is: What's holding you back from believing and receiving the truth of who God called you to be? There are a myriad of descriptions of who Christ says you are, even as satan tries to affirm you as himself. Deceiving many and turning them away from the Lord, it is his job to get you off course and hinder you from receiving God's perfection for your life.

The Bible declares that satan is a liar and the father of them. In essence, John 10:10 calls him the thief that comes to steal, kill, and to destroy. Let's take a look at the afflictions presented and inflicted by the enemy. They are: wounds, pain, and hurt.

What is a wound?
What is pain?
What is hurt?

Merriam-Webster defines the three specifically
relative to each other. As I paraphrase, Webster
by its entrance definition of each is written:

Wound is injury to the physical being caused by breaking of the skin and bleeding.

Pain is defined as an uncomfortable sensation, the feeling of ache.

Hurt is the action of causing or inflicting pain.

Your complete breakthrough will only come when you have proven to God that your faith is unaltered by the effects of hardships. Active prayer, praise and worship, and the wait for the promise are methods used in order to obtain advancement. Normally, infants are only birthed after nine months of pregnancy. Generally, the beginning of the pregnancy is described to be felt with a lot of morning sickness, crying and regurgitating. Although the first stages of the process seem so difficult, we must always focus on the promise.

The beautiful baby that is being formed in the womb is developing through the process of change. Even through birth, the pains of labor are extremely intensified as you get close to delivering. Even John 16:21 says: *"A woman when she is in travail hath sorrow, because her hour is come: but as soon as she is delivered of the child, remembereth no more the anguish, for joy that a man is born into the world."* Also, Romans 8:28 declares this and reads: *"And we know that all things work together for good to them that love God, to them who are the called according to his purpose."* So I say to you, receive and rejoice in what God allows because it is working on your behalf to repair and restore you for the inevitable transformation of the new you. No longer will you internalize your hurt, pain, or rejection. It is time for you to move forward.

Now is this relative to what happens when you put one foot forward? Even in those instances when it feels that you have taken two steps backward, the good news is, *God Restores what*

Remains. Man get back up! Women stand strong! God is only tearing you down to build you back up. As frustrating as it may be, He is even going to reshape your character. If you allow Him to shape you into the character of His Son, you can begin to operate in your inheritance. For the Lord knows when and how to rescue you! So, do yourself justice by doing this preparation for your transformation.

Take a minute to **sit up, inhale, exhale, release, and** now **relax!** You are now ready to embark upon your divine destiny. Just as every sentence begins with capital letters and ends with punctuation, life has commas, periods, exclamation points, and question marks. Learning to connect the dots in the middle of a breaking can be pleasurable when you set goals, follow through, and expect rewarding benefits. As we continue to engage in prayer at the end of each chapter, may the puzzles of your life connect piece by piece

Prayer:

Father God, thank you for reconstructing my life. Lead me to the rock that's higher than my imagination. Keep my mind focused on your promises only. In Jesus name,

Amen

CHAPTER THREE

I AM, WHO GOD SAYS I AM

I AM A CONQUEROR

Who does Christ say I am? The Bible encompasses well over hundreds of descriptive Scriptures that affirm who I am in Christ Jesus! Therefore, I am who God says I am! Say it out loud and let the devil hear you declare your righteousness through Jesus Christ. Watchman Nee, said and I quote, ***"Outside of Christ, I am weak; inside of Christ I am strong."*** (2014). The Bible reads ***"I am crucified with Christ: nevertheless I live; yet not I, but Christ liveth in me: and the life which I now live in the flesh I live by the faith of the Son of God, who loved me, and gave himself for me."*** (Gal. 2:20).

Because of your faith in God, that of your old nature is pruned and cast out. You become new creations through His blood sacrifice on Calvary's Cross. In this sense, Christ is the One who internally uses the vessel in which He resides to glorify His name through our daily actions. Living completely dependent on Christ, while acknowledging the Word of the Gospel as guidance in the form of a template is how God intended us to live. This can be recognized in those who have been "Born Again"

The fact is that when we accept Christ, the spirit of our inner being is awakened. This transformation is another one of God's breaking processes for change and restoration. When the inner being is awakened, you can clearly see things in light of His guidance for your total makeover. The accountability starts with acknowledging that you need to be changed. Once your confession is made, you now can encounter the change as the process of transformation begins.

Needless to say, when we are broken, we are simply without the healing manifestation that Christ offers. Then it becomes this endless cycle of manufacturing broken people. Why? Broken people break people, and hurt people hurt people. You see, Jesus wants to live **in** us so that He may live **through** us. God created the world so that He may experience communion with man. However, complete communion cannot come from a broken vessel. Of course, broken vessels lead to dysfunctional behavior.

Since God cannot dwell in an unclean temple, we must submit to the process of becoming sanctified or set apart.

The Lord spoke to Jeremiah saying: ***"Before I formed you in the belly or womb, I KNEW THEE and before you were born, I SET YOU APART"...*** (Jer. 1:5 with emphasis added). Even before the foundations of the world, God knew the plan for each of our lives. Yet, He gives us the freedom to choose good or evil? When you come into the awareness of whom the Potter created for His pleasures, you become committed to choosing good over evil, righteousness over sin, love over hatred, and integrity over dishonesty. Making godly choices are all indications of knowing who you are.

Since God is good and righteous, and since He is the epitome of love and integrity, you are who He is, simple as that. Therefore, His purpose for your life is perfect. Because He embodies total perfection, He desires the best for His child. He is such a caring Father that He knows you by name and knows the numbers of every hair on your head. He is such a faithful Father that His "child support" is second to none. As a matter of fact, 2 Timothy 2:13 emphasizes that ***"He cannot deny Himself."*** A real father does not disown his child. Thus, Philippians 4:19 gives us the assurance that ***"God SHALL supply ALL of our need according to His riches in glory by Christ Jesus!"***

A powerful analogy in Scripture which refers to our transformation in becoming new creatures in Christ is, Isaiah 64:8: ***"But now, O LORD, Thou art our Father; we are the clay, and Thou our Potter; and we all are the work of Thy hand."*** When we become clay in the Potter's hand, we must allow Him not only to mold us, but to create in us a clean heart. This is the earnest prayer of David, even after he sinned against God. The reason why David could pray like this is that he was in awe of God. ***"Stand in awe, and sin not: commune with your own heart upon your bed, and be still. Selah"*** (Psa. 4:4).

We continue to fall, either by thought, word or deed because we have no sense of awe. What is awe but a profound fascination with the grandeur and majesty of God? Once we come into a revelation of who and what God actually is, and who we truly are in Him, sin and its attending enchantments will no longer fascinate us. Indeed, awe of God is the antidote to sin and brokenness!

Even in the midst of this "incubator" process, God has a way of shielding you during the darkest and deepest pits of your life. Allow the prayers and testimonies of those that David shares in the Psalms to help affirm your true development in Christ. Keep in mind that satan even tried to tempt Jesus after 40 days and 40 nights of consecration in the wilderness. But He resisted every alternative gift of wickedness that satan had to offer.

In 1 Corinthians 10:13, the Word says: *"There hath no temptation taken you but such as is common to man: but God is faithful, who will not suffer you to be tempted above that ye are able; but will with the temptation also make a way to escape, that ye may be able to bear it."* Since God recognizes that we are all mere vessels, in need of His touch, the temptations we face are of no secret to Him. The painful process of being broken and allowing God to repair us, enables us to reflect on where we are in relation to how far we have come.

At the end of the day, the Bible boldly declares that we are " *fearfully and wonderfully made."* The thing to do at this point is to accept what He says. Say it out loud with me: "I AM, WHO GOD SAYS I AM! *"Nay, in ALL things we are more than conquerors through Him that loved us"* (Rom. 8:37 with emphasis added).

I am a warrior.
"I am the righteousness of God."
I am better now. "*No weapon formed*
against me shall prosper!"

Prayer:

Father God, in the name of Jesus, teach me your ways and lead me in the right path. Order each step I take only to give your name glory. In Jesus name,

Amen

CHAPTER FOUR

FAKING THROUGH
THE BREAKING

HIDING BEHIND THE PAIN

Oftentimes, many tears are shed and camouflaged behind a fake facade because you don't want to be labeled as weak by humans who tend to be judgmental by nature. Many of them do not willfully inflict pain, but as I stated earlier, "hurt people hurt people" due to their hurts and insecurities. So then, cover-ups on both sides become sporadic, and even dysfunctional. This is a barrier or wall that people often build to fake through the breaking and pretend that they are **OKAY.** In all actuality it's far from the truth!

As we see with the Psalmist David, brokenness, despondency, and aloneness is what triggers the repair that leads to transformation. In my opinion, the humbleness of a healed heart blooms a new life. Inner life and beauty can genuinely flourish when it comes out of a broken heart that has been healed. The process of being broken and then repaired reveals the rewards of standing in the midst of the fire while maintaining a straight face. *"But the God of all grace, who hath called us unto His eternal glory by Christ Jesus, after that ye have suffered a while, make you perfect, stablish, strengthen, settle you."* Now that's a promise found in 1 Peter 5:10.

SPIRITUAL NUGGET

God breaks us, because of his love for us. When we comprehend and clear our heads after the breaking, the ashes and residue becomes beautiful. Needless to say, we must realize and take in account, that spoiling our child without discipline, is the act of not really loving them completely. The Bible says, God chasten whom He loves. It reads, *"My son, despise not the chastening of the Lord; neither be weary of his correction: For whom the Lord loves He corrects, even as a father correcteth the son in whom he delighteth."* (Prov. 3:11-12). Remember, We are *"BROKEN TO*

BE REPAIRED" for preparation in the Kingdom of God. He loves us and will never leave us broken!

I cannot **emphasize** enough that God corrects us because of His **love** for **us.** Let me say this again, "Spoiling our child without discipline is the act of not really loving them completely." I must repeat this powerful scripture too. According to, Proverbs 3:11-12, it offers this commentary: ***"My son, despise not the chastening of the LORD; neither be weary of His correction: For whom the LORD loveth he correcteth; even as a father the son in whom he delighteth."*** A biblical truth and the crux of the matter is that we must be corrected when we are wrong so that we are not left dysfunctional in our behaviors! Here is a nugget worth remembering: we are ***"BROKEN TO BE REPAIRED;"*** then we are PAUSED ON PURPOSE, so that we are PREPARED for PROMISE .

If you can just clear your head after the breaking and finally comprehend that your "pause" was on purpose, even in this season of Covid-19. One of the promises that comes to mind is found in Isaiah 61:3: ***"To appoint unto them that mourn in Zion, to give unto them beauty for ashes, the oil of joy for mourning, the garment of praise for the spirit of heaviness; that they might be called trees of righteousness, the planting of the LORD, that He might be glorified."***

Surely, we all have been or are still cracked pots! Even as all of us are broken in some way or another, there is hope for the weary, the wounded, the broken, and the sad. Jesus wants to heal us where we hurt, but we must stop hiding in the trenches. We can be participators in the process, but we must avoid being codependent. Stop trying to fix yourself and admit that you are nothing but clay in the Potter's hand. If you are struggling and desperately need the comfort and encouragement from the Lord, just take a moment and ask Him to help. All he needs is your permission to reconstruct your path. So I say to you, allow Him to mold you as you focus on enduring the process and moving forward in the things of God. Refuse to be like Lot's wife who looked back into her past and became a ***pillar of salt*** (Gen. 19:26). Rather, keep in mind that "***The joy of the Lord is your strength***" (Neh. 8:10 c), and the God of all peace shall reward your faithfulness in due season.

Frequently, many people look back and allow the past to immobilize them from moving into the promised place that our Father has prepared for us. But if you are an example for those who are watching your life, they will learn by your faith how to hold on, even in the midst of a "breaking." Instead of looking back at who caused your pain, try forgiving those who helped you to grow.

I have learned that you can't just look at a person and size them up. You couldn't even imagine what it took for many of us to grow to the place where we are in God. Let me speak for myself; I didn't get here by osmosis. When I chose to stop hiding behind my pain and decided to endure the "breaking," God was faithful in keeping His Word. God has given to every man "***A measure of faith***;" however, our faith can only be strengthened by reading and trusting His Word. ***"For whatsoever things were written aforetime were written for our learning, that we through patience and comfort of the Scriptures might have hope"*** (Rom. 15:4).

Even in areas of hardship, if you can't see the hand of God moving, just believe that he will bring you through the most crucial times.

The Word alone is able to purify your mind from all doubt, transform your weak will into a will of steel, and completely heal every one of your damaged emotions. That's why the devil spends the bulk of his time attempting to distract you from the Word."

The point is: your response in the storm determines how long you'll stay in it. But the power of response is established through the Word. Your response will either keep you broken or help make you stronger. In your weakness, your strength is birthed. Impatience can cause you to miss out on God's perfect timing and his will. God will always make you wait in circumstances because they are not ready for you and you are not ready for them. Manifestation that is delayed is not manifestation denied. You must trust the timing to be accurate.

Imagine sitting at the lake and casting your reel. You must wait on a fish to bite before you can reel him in. An impatient fisherman never catches a fish. That is just like the old saying by Vince Lombardi, "A winner never quits and a quitter never wins." Every tear you shed, every sleepless night, every clean and unclean thought, every mistake, and disappointment, God is always with you through the wait. He awaits our repentance during the breaking period. Therefore, why can't we wait for His perfect will to be done in our lives? You must believe that God is with us, and God is for us! You must be patient. There is a saying that, *"good things come to those who wait."*

The natural things that you plan won't happen immediately. But as time approaches when your destiny shall be fulfilled, the manifestation shall surely come for what you are believing God for. The things you are waiting for will not be a day under due or overdue as long as you trust in God's timing. Because he is the creator of time. He is time. And he has time to wrap up the evolving process as he stretches your faith. During waiting periods, God is building your character and faith through your journey of life. Trust in him to exalt you in time when you are willing to wait on his plan for your life.

A very strong side note is that you must learn how to forgive and not to blame others for your failures and disappointments.

I encourage you to be thankful for their role in your maturity! When the dirt is thrown on top of you, it's OK! Why? You are a seed planted and you are about to spring up out of the dirt and grow! You are being broken for repair. Instead, seek God for restoration. Look at it like this. We have all battled with some type of challenge or weakness in our life. But because of God's mercy and grace you are able to withstand the breaking process. The test becomes a testimony and those whose see the victory will be encouraged to hold on as well. During the trials that test your faith, you must stay focused in the Word of God.

You must stand strong believing that God will do what he said. I can attest that Jesus is a keeper, a comforter, and the closest friend you'll ever need. When you've done all you can do, and there's nowhere to turn, you stand still and let God's plan unfold in your life. He knows our end from our beginning. Time has a way of bringing about change in circumstances. These opportunities are given to us all. It is what you are willing to pursue to achieve your dreams and fulfill your God intended purpose.

1 Peter 4:12-13 reads *"**Beloved, think it not strange concerning the fiery trial which is to try you, as though some strange thing has happened unto you.**" "**...But rejoice inasmuch as ye are partakers of Christ's sufferings; that, when his glory shall be reviled, ye may be glad also with exceeding joy.**"* You must open up and receive the love that only the Anointed One, Jesus our Savior can give. He wants to give His LOVE to all who will accept HIM.

WINGS OF BEAUTY
BROKEN TO BE REPAIRED
EXPECT HEALING IN THE PROCESS OF CHANGE

Have you ever felt like the clock stopped ticking in your life? Well I encourage you to keep moving. Do not give up! Don't throw in the towel yet! Rewind the clock if you must but keep pressing forward. As you know time has a way of channeling the path to your destiny. We will not all arrive at the same time, but we will get there as we persevere. Get up and turn the time clock back on. Every time it seems to stop, turn it back on or wind it up.

If you are sitting alone ask yourself, "What can I do while I am here?" Start by digging deep within to find that broken place where you lost your confidence during your journey. I know it seems like a great battle every day. Let me say, you have what it takes to succeed. The Bible tells you, *"I can do all things through Christ who strengthens me."* (Phil. 4:13). It may not be easy. However, it is possible! The brokenness is a place where now you stand up and take charge and allow God to lead again.

We can open the eyes of our youth, women, and men to break the silence of what's going on behind the scenes. The things that are hindering their ability to walk in their divine destiny will be revealed. Stop being afraid of what the natural eye sees or believes as truth. It's time to take a risk. So what if you fail. Get back up and try again. Failure is not failure without a fight. As I tell my children, " Get your fight back!" It's time to appreciate who you are.

Healing is a process of breaking down the barriers of deceptions that weaken the mind. It enables you to change your mind-set, so that you may become who you really are. God has the perfect plan and the delivering power to set us free from bondage and fear. Fear is the binding grip that terminates the enthusiasm of the inner spirit to rise up and be bold. Now here is where you unleash the cannon of fire from God. When you thought you were alone God was always there. Song writer said, *"He was there all the time."* Not only there all the time but, he is right here right now all the time. So your clock is ticking and you still have time to evolve.

Playing the role	**Saving Face**

The scab slowly heals by each layer of skin, from inside out. That's how the Lord wants to heal us. Our inner being must be illuminated in-order for change to take place. Although you see the wound as a place of injury and never see the healing doesn't mean it's not taking place. The constant removal of the protective scab prolongs the healing. Why inflict yourself over and over? Break the cycle and yield to the breaking or crushing process of change.

I recall that every-time I pulled the scab off over and over again, I re-injured myself. Self infliction is as cruel as the grave. You become addictive to the pain. Why? You hid behind the insecurities and the fear of rejection. The scab will not heal if you keep picking at it. Call me a picker. Start here and prepare your wound for its healing. If we continue to interfere with God's process of the breaking we can't be repaired.

You must take your hands off and allow the healing to be completed.

Not just to take place but to finish its course. Take the time to heal.

Locked in a shell

Are you afraid of what they think of you? Do you find yourself isolating from everyone around you? How can you move past the wound, the hurt, the pain? There is a key to transparency. Tell your story in increments, no one can handle your life all at once. As your experiences are released a healing should take place, for both you and the listener.

Life happens to us all. Each venture, whether good or bad, is beneficial to enlighten us along the way. A fisherman does not open his worms before he gets to the fishing hole. So be careful in releasing too much too soon. No one wants to let the wild cat out of the bag, if it's going to claw or attack viciously! Being sensitive to what to share at the right time will encourage the brokenness in another individual. The bible says, *"Two are better than one".* (Eccles. 4:9 *a) "And that iron sharpened iron."* (Prov. 27:17 a).

Hiding behind the smiles and bleeding at the same time

The pain of rejection is a constant reminder the enemy replays in your mind that you are not wanted or how bad you look. You hide behind your smiles and pretend to be happy. As insecure beings, we need restoration from the inside out. The feeling of rejection is the enemy's way of keeping you isolated and bound. It keeps you from communicating with family and friends. This is where God steps in and heals the brokenhearted. His word validates who you really are. Not satan. Even during the period of feeling despondent you still have a choice to make. You can get up and fight back.

The choices you make are decisions you have to deal with. God gives each one of us a free will. When you are being rejected you have to be the one to get up. Rejection as Webster would define is, it could mean pushing someone away or keeping something back from the person. It results in you becoming an introvert. That's just like you offered me a gift and I don't receive it. Then I am rejecting your generosity.

Jesus faced rejection even in his own country; they did not receive him well. It's a matter of if you decide to accept yourself. Jesus knew who he was and his purpose plan from God. You must find the ability to accept and appreciate who God created you to be. You are unique! There is only one like you. Admire who you are and not allow people to dictate your worth. Now answer your fear through your faith in God's repairing your brokenness, because He has **A perfect plan for your purpose in the breaking process.** The Bible affirms. "**That *the steps of a good man are ordered by the Lord: and he delighteth in his way.*"** (Ps 37:23). David also inquires of the Lord to keep him in his sight for protection through adversity. Scripture says in Psalms 17:8.. "*Keep me as the apple of the eye, hide me under the shadow of thy wings,*".....

Lord teach me to wait as you prepare me for my miracle.

Scripture says, "*If ye abide in me, and my words abide in you, ye shall ask what ye will, and it shall be done unto you.*" (John 15:7).

Prayer:

Father in the name of Jesus, open my understanding and teach me how to love as you desire. I thank you for working everything out for my good. And because of the breaking, I will grow stronger and more equipped to stand in the face of my adversities.

Amen

CHAPTER FIVE

PERSEVERANCE

STAY IN THE RACE

Jesus is the epitome of a true warrior! Our Savior. Our King. Our Lord. Our Strength. Our Hope. Our Peace. As a matter of fact, let's make this clear. The Bible says in Acts 4:12...***"Neither is there salvation in any other, for there is none other name under heaven given among men, whereby we must be saved."*** Paul talks about the race that we all should contend in. That is to run it with patience. Although he suffered struggles while preaching the gospel of Jesus Christ, Paul persevered through it all. He encouraged Timothy to stay focused and do the same.

Even when persecution comes, stay in the race. Keep your eyes on the positive aspects of this life where we hope in the Advocate's deliverance from all earthly affairs. In 1 Corinthians 9:24-27 Paul says this; "***Know ye not that they which run in a race run all, but one receiveth the prize? So run, that ye may obtain. And every man that striveth for the mastery is temperate in all things. Now they do it to obtain a corruptible crown; but we an incorruptible. I therefore so run, not as uncertainly; so fight I, not as one that beateth the air:But I keep under my body, and bring it into subjection: lest that by any means, when I have preached to others, I myself should be a castaway.***"Listen, what Paul wants the body of believers to understand is simple. If you are going to run in a physical race, prepare your body to endure pain and suffering to gain the win! Paul's analogy is geared towards our faith in contending with the pressures of this world. He teaches us to train our spiritual man through prayer, fasting, and thanksgiving unto God. We all must lay down the sins that make us fail. In doing so, God can catapult you through the breaking and repairing process to help you heal even when you think all is lost.

However, our focus should be on the eternal crown that comes from the Lord. Constantly seeking the things above, rather than laying hold of things on earth. All of which will rust and rot. It's good to have things, but don't allow them to become idols before God. Let us keep our eyes on Jesus. Yes, Life has its twists and turns, but only one path is the right one. Clearly, Jesus is the way to The Father! He said to the disciples after the last supper, ***"I am the way, the truth, and the life: No one cometh unto the Father, but by me."*** (John 14:6).

Wilma Rudolph said and I quote; "The Triumph can't be had without the struggle." (n/d). There are obstacles in our paths gearing us to fail. Unfortunately, we can't bypass them all without enduring some hardship. Wilma was told that she would never walk again after being diagnosed with polio. Doctors gave her devastating news that she would not walk again nor live a normal life. However, she believed in the report of the Lord. Her faith moved the mountain out of her way! Wilma became the "first American woman to win in the Olympics. She obtained three gold medals in a single game of track and field." (Norwood, 2017). What an amazing comeback after a devastating setback! Believe me, You can and you will get through the most challenging downfalls in your life. It's just a setup for you to bounce back. That's when a level of faith should arise from your inner depths and say, "I will get through this! No one and nothing shall move my faith. I assure you, the same God that brought you out before, is the same God that will bring you out again! Because the Bible says, ***"Jesus Christ is the same yesterday, today, and for ever."*** (Heb. 13:8).

Therefore you should Stay in the RACE! In the end, you will WIN! It is not to the one who runs the fastest, nor the strongest. However, the one who will endure the process shall be saved when tested in the fiery trial. Hebrews 12:1-2... ***"Wherefore seeing we also are compassed about with so great a cloud of witnesses, let us lay aside every weight, and the sin which doth so easily beset***

us, and let us run with patience the race that is set before us,
Looking unto Jesus the author and finisher of our faith; who
for the joy that was set before him endured the cross, despising
the shame, and is set down at the right hand of the throne
of God.".

Stay on course

And in some instances you may have to set boundaries. Over the course of time you learn to set walls between you and what keeps you from the promises that God has for you. Continue to try and walk as he leads every step. Oftentimes we try to hold on to those around us just because of familiarity. After which when you release the things that God is telling you to release, you can see that the boundaries made sense. Then you could move on into your destiny.

I know it's hard sometimes to walk away from those that have been in your life forever. Nevertheless, God will bring new Associates that can help Propel you to your destiny. We have to work together in order to form a union that brings unity in the body of Christ. That's the way the Lord works with us. He wants us to work together as he works with us. You must find a way to continue to open your heart and mind to the will of God. So that when it's displayed that you will see it openly and move toward what God is saying for you to do. Giving an account, if you want your life to change, you must be momentarily uncomfortable.

The breaking that the father does is not to hinder you or to stop your progress, but they help heal you in the areas that need healing. We are broken but we don't know we're broken. That's why we have to accept the healing that comes from the Lord. God wants to transform our hearts and our minds. If we would only be transparent and open up and say that I need help, then can you receive the help that you need and accept the healing that God has for you.

Others have always walked around saying that they're okay, smiling saying it's good, but it's really not, need I say it again. You must be honest with yourself, you have to look in the mirror and say it is time for a change. I see my Silhouette. I see my reflection. I see what I look like. I see what I want to be. But now, how can I accomplish that? So now I am on this journey. Knowing that the Lord has a plan for my life and I have to be the one and the only one that can accept that change.

During the transformation there's going to be pain, there's going to be rejection, there's going to be opposition. After all, the Lord is with you through every trial. So settle yourself in and know that the Lord will not leave you nor forsake you and he will never stop loving you. He has come to give you and I an abundant life but you have to be the one to make the decision to change. During the process you have to change your heart toward him, then and only then can the healing take place.

In the breaking, there will be healing as you go through each trial that has come to make you strong and build your faith in God. Our faith is what is used in order to get us from one place to another. The bible says, *"But without faith it is impossible to please him: for he that cometh to God must believe that he is, and that he is a rewarder of them that diligently seek him."* (Heb. 11:6). You have to believe in his healing power inorder to receive it. Faith will most definitely help you in remaining calm as you are reconstructed by God. You must endure the process of change to be completely restored. Be sure to Hold firm to what you believe and you can make it through the hard times of challenges and the storms of life.

Listen to this, take for instance if you want to charge or jump start someone's battery. You would not put the positive and negative connections together. It takes a positive to positive and negative to negative connection to bring the source of power you need to start the car. So then you would connect the positive cable to positive cable and negative cable to one negative of the live battery and the dead battery the cable negative to a piece of metal on the car. If you make a mistake in connecting them the wrong way, you will ignite a fuse spark or a battery explosion! This is a way the enemy tries to distract your judgment in decision making. Stay focused.

Now I know the bible says,"**Iron sharpens Iron**," but only when we work together. See the positive and negative works jointly to supply the energy needed to give or generate the boost. That's why it is so important to stay on course and apply positive energy in negative situations. If you are looking for validation from people or a pat on the back, let me let you in on a very significant observation. **Jesus** is the **SOURCE**! When you connect to his power you have the power to overcome the obstacles on your journey of restoration. Then Cry out to God, because He is the only one who can heal you. Open up and receive your deliverance as it will come every day when you invite him into your life. The understanding is that you have to be the one to invite him in. He is a gentleman and will not go against your will. Jesus does give free will to us all. In Deuteronomy 30:19 God says, *"I call heaven and earth to record this day against you, [that] I have set before you life and death, blessing and cursing: therefore choose life, that both thou and thy seed may live."*

As you recognize the power and authority given to you then you are well on your way to being renewed in the fullness of God's transforming grace.

Prayer:

Father in the name of Jesus, I ask you to give me the strength I need to stay strong during the testing of my faith. Give me the tools and wisdom to conquer hardship during the trials. Teach me how to stay on course. I accept the authority given to me and use it to speak according to your word that I am being empowered by your spirit, In Jesus name.

Amen

CHAPTER SIX

EMBRACING THE NEW YOU

DON'T BURY ME YET

The beauty of it all is that you appreciate and embrace what caused your new you. Afflictions of your past should not remind you of how bad it hurt or how horrible it was to go through that season in your life. However, when you cast down imaginations which cause you to fail or relapse, you see the new you developing for your future. Because of your receptiveness and acceptance of the fact that God is a healer, healing is currently taking place. You see, no one wants to be buried before their time whether it is by physical or spiritual death.

This is why you cannot allow your thoughts to overpower you with the negative assumptions the enemy tries to suppress about you. Just as David asked the Lord to keep him as the apple of his eye, we need the same mentality. Knowing we are the very focus of God he won't let us fall. And even when you have a set-back he will pick you up.

The daily affirmations you make between you and God will develop the new you. So embrace all of it! Every bit of it! Every sleepless night, every tear you've shed, every form of rejection, every wound, every hurt, and every pain that caused your demise, embrace it in its entirety. Yes! Another thing to be excited about is why it happened. It has catapulted you to your now, and will take you to your next! Just begin to thank God for every trial which came to make you strong. You see, it is within the trials that we face and have to endure, that we are built through the process of breaking and repairing. Most of all, appreciate and celebrate them all. You are now Destined for Greatness! God says "You are his ***beloved***." We all have things that we've dealt with by either the wrong or right decisions we made.

Subsequently, it made us who we are. Whether wrong or right the consequences we suffered helped mold and shape us. In essence, your healing is activated through every challenge you face. Mainly, for your redemption to live out your destiny with confidence in the Lord's healing and restoration for your body, mind, and soul. The bible tells of all our heroic ancestors which suffered in trials and recovered through their victories. Which were written for our hope in Jesus Christ and his vindication for us?

Therefore, no matter what has happened to you it does not define who you are. You are who God says you are, plain and simple. No matter how people try to define you through your past, it is the victories accomplished through hope that do so. Hoping you would come out of the situation you were in, it made no difference whether you were saved or not. You hoped you would survive the persecution. Well let me tell you this, every Haman in your life will hang themselves. Including the python who no longer desires to constrict you, but now tries to swallow you whole will expose himself! I assure you everything in this season the enemy plotted against you will not prosper. He will slip up and uncover himself. You will see the ambush coming. No longer will you be deceived!

After taking a close look at Genesis 29:17-35, Laban deceived Jacob into marrying Leah, causing her heart to be broken. Therefore, causing Jacob to labor seven years to get the promised bride, Rachel. The trickster got tricked! *"Whatever you sow you will reap."* You will face the repercussions, so be careful in what seeds you sow. Jacob had a seasonal waiting period to marry the girl of his dreams after the deception of his brother Esau. During the time of his waiting to marry Racheal, Leah conceived a son. God's favor was upon her in the brokenness of her heart. In her misery, she thought Jacob's love would turn after the birth of her child.

However, she was wounded, hurt, and in a painful state. Her act of faith in God made her assume it would turn Jacob's heart towards her. Continually, his passion and determination grew vigorously more for Rachel. This time is a reality check for Leah.

Feeling unwanted and unloved in her conceptions of the first four sons she named her sons according to her pain.

In verses 32-35, she gets revelation of how to touch God's heart! Take a look at the names she gave each son. In verse 32 it reads, *"And Leah conceived, and bore a son, and called his name Reuben: for she said, Surely the Lord looked upon my affliction: now therefore my husband will love me.* **It is because the Lord has seen my misery.** The Name **Reuben** means, "**Behold a son**!" Verse 33 entails, continual pain and brokenness for Leah. It says, *"And she conceived again, and bore a son: and said, Because the Lord hath heard I was hated, I am not loved! He hath therefore given me this son also: and she called his name Simeon."* **His name means To Hear!** Verse 34 states; *"And she conceived again, and bare a son; and said, Now this time will my husband be joined unto me, because I have born him three sons: therefore was his name called Levi.*

Levi means, Joined or Connected! Still through her suffering Leah's pain went unnoticed by Jacob. All he could see or focus on was his beloved Rachel!

Lastly, in verse 35, here we see Leah aligning her faith to purpose! God rewards her in spirit with another son. It says, *"And She conceived again, and bore a son: and she said, "Now will I PRAISE the Lord." therefore she called his name Judah; and left bearing."* The Bible reveals that Leah's pain connected her to her **praise**!

God revealed to me the significance of Leah's first four sons. Meaning, **"Behold a son to hear joined and connected to Praise!"** You and I can relate to the rejection Leah felt throughout this time of testing. Her faith in God grew beyond the desire to receive Jacob's love. Oftentimes, you look continually at the circumstances rather than to God. If I could sum this up in a few words for you, It is simply this, **"DON'T BURY ME YET!"** In the midst of my pain the weight I carry belongs to the Lord. He tells us in his word to cast our cares upon him. Rightfully, knowing that it will benefit you in the end.

The plan God has for us is greater than you can imagine! Leah's life was strategically planned by God's divine purpose. Without Leah God revealed to me that there would be no Messiah without her lineage through Judah. See **Judah's lineage** lineup was **Leah, Judah, David**, and then our blessed **Messiah "Yeshua."** Jesus came through the birthing canal from Leah's lineage! Now that in itself is a powerful observation. I am blessed to know that Leah giving birth to **Judah** made it possible for the Tribe of Judah to birth David's lineage, and the coming of our Savior Jesus Christ. Leah is known as the *Foremother* of our Messiah.

I can hear you at this point saying, "**DON'T BURY ME YET!**" It's not over for you. It is not over until God says it's over! God has a perfect plan for the lives of his people. Being broken is a good place to humble yourself before God. As you see, the purpose of Leah's pain was necessary! And there is purpose in your pain. Healing can only take place during and after the pain. Listen, Leah gave Jacob 6 sons and a daughter.

Although, Rachel had Jacob's heart. Leah was honoured in his death. The bible tells us that Rachel died giving birth to Benjamin. He was Jacob's youngest son and last son. She was buried in a roadside grave on their way to Bethlehem. And there her body stayed. Genesis 49:29 says Jacob's last request of his sons was *"I am to be gathered unto my people: bury me with my fathers in the cave......* verse 31 **says** *"There they buried Abraham and Sarah his wife; there they buried Isaac and Rebekah his wife; and there I buried Leah."* The reason why you cannot allow the enemy to distract you from God's purpose is this, the breaking comes before the healing. Leah was broken but repaired with her relationship with God.

What an honor it was for Leah to be buried in the ancestral tomb. In today's respect, Leah was not acknowledged as a woman of beauty. However, the birth of Judah fulfilled her spectacular purpose. Psalms 115:12 (a) tells us, *"The Lord has been mindful of us:"* …. God will restore you during the process of change.

I recall a message Jesus gave me concerning getting rid of my daily fleshly desires. He asked if I would seek his divine will for my life. As he reminded me that he would restore life from the death of sin, in exchange for his godly desires. The Lord promised that he would resuscitate me. I continued to listen as he whispered to me, **"Just breathe**." Then I opened up and released a deep breath.

Now, here I am trying to make sense of why I had to hold my breath while going through storms in my life. When fear grips your heart The Lord has to open your eyes so you will discern his directions. He explained to me about the process of resuscitation. Which is *"the action or process of reviving someone from unconsciousness or apparent death."* (Merriam-Webster, 2020). The doctor usually asks when someone has a heart attack, stroke, or stop breathing, if they would like the person to be resuscitated? And in emergencies, they will automatically perform the process to restore life. They jump-start your heart. Jesus wants to revive you totally in wholeness, spirit, mind, body, and soul. If you submit to a spiritual jump-start you will be repaired. We are all born and conceived in sin. No one is exempt. If for one moment you stop judging and look in the mirror at who's looking back at you. You can walk in full recovery. During this stage of learning, it is an important lesson. God spoke and said, "Let me breathe for you." The resuscitation he wants to complete in our life is he blows his breath on us and awakens the spirit in us.

As he continued the conversation with me, he gave me the spiritual meaning of **CPR**. It is **CHRIST'S PROMISED REDEMPTION.** Jesus promised to redeem you when you turn from your ways to his. Therefore, when you allow God to break the barriers of unbelief and rebellion of human nature he restores the spirit to man. See when you abandon yourself, Jesus is there to resuscitate you!

If we stop trying to do it ourselves and allow God to break every part of us that's not like him, we will survive. Your perspective has to change as well as your perception. You must begin to look through the lens of God as he sees you. **CPR** is guaranteed when you surrender all unto the Lord. Receive the love of God as he loves you unconditionally. Even when you try to hide or turn away from God, he comes after you, that's **CHRIST'S PROMISED REDEMPTION!**

The Bible says in Luke 19:10, *"**For The son of man is come to seek and to save that which was lost.**"* You are His treasured masterpiece. The BIBLE clearly states in Zephaniah 3:17, *"**The Lord thy God in the midst of thee is mighty; he will save, he will rejoice over thee with joy; he will rest in his love, he will joy over thee with singing**."*

Reference to Luke chapter 15, it states the moral: to the lost sheep every one of us is very precious in the sight of the Lord. If even one is lost, He will leave the 99 to find and restore the one. He loves us all the same. *"**He has no respecter of person**."* (Rom. 2:11). If you find it hard to embrace His love, you are out of alignment and out of the agreement between his purpose and your destiny. To have contentment and peace, you must agree with His love for you. Then learn to love yourself. Stop sabotaging yourself. Your worth is far greater than rubies, pearls, and diamonds.

Receive this freely, **CPR, Christ's Promised Redemption**. Understand Christ preordained to heal and save you! His blood covenant made it all possible. Remember you are his creation *"**Broken to be Repaired**"* only through and by him. Instead of focusing on your circumstances, focus on the only one who heals, delivers, and sets you free from bondage. His name is **Jesus**.

Although Hanna was barren, her focus became fixed on the Lord. She made her petition to God and left it in his hands. Sometimes you have to release the burden to the Lord and let it go. In your brokenness, you will be resuscitated. You do not have to compromise with the evil one to gain acceptance, attention or validation from him. God has made you uniquely designed on purpose. You are Destined to be Great!

Stop right now in comparing yourself to everyone else. The Lord said he is pleased with you just the way you are and is willing to resurrect those dead places in your life. Yes, the dry bones can live! He will make you whole. You are identified through Christ. In your weaknesses, his grace is sufficient for you. When you feel like throwing in the towel, don't do it! You are made for this.

Psalm 37: 23-24 assures us that; "*The steps of a good man are ordered by the Lord and he delighted in his way. Though he fall, he shall not be utterly cast down, for the Lord upholdeth him with his hand.*" See, through all of this God is defending you. He said, I have heard your prayers and seen your cries! He is concerned about what makes you happy and what makes you sad. What makes you weep, makes him weep. What offends you, offends him. You are not alone in your journey. Stand still and know that he will not let you fall. And if you do he will carry you!

You know the picture you see of a set of footprints in the sand, it lets us know these are the times when he carried you!! Even when others harshly mistreat or mishandle you, "I will vindicate you", says the Lord. Your recovery during the breaking process proves that you contain the strength that you didn't know was there. Honey, you are built for this season of your life. Go forward!

Keep moving. Be encouraged. Keep your eyes on Jesus. If nothing else let the enemy know that there is nothing that can separate you from Christ. The enemy wants you to fail, but as Jesus prayed for Peter's faith to fail him not, he has prayed for you too my friend. Remember you are exactly where you are supposed to be. You are a light to those who are lost by darkness and engulfed in sin. When People observe your lifestyle they are convicted to live a better life. So don't you dare quit!! Their healing and deliverance depend on your walk with the Lord. This may be as close as they come to a church service or a preacher. I encourage you to keep moving forward. Because of God's miraculous works I have been able to live in confidence and obedience as he is processing me.

Prayer:

Father, in the name of Jesus, we ask that you will instruct us on how to embrace the process of change and strengthen us during the purging of our old self. Thank you for your sovereign love and blood sacrifice. Which makes us freed of our sinful nature as we give our hearts to you through repentance. We honor you for all you have delivered us from in past trials and those to come. Thank you Lord for resuscitating us and giving us your divine **CPR, Christ's Promised Redemption** *that we will live out our purpose according to your will. In Jesus name,*

Amen

CHAPTER SEVEN

PICK UP THE PIECES AND MOVE FORWARD

LIVING OUT YOUR PURPOSE

Remember when transitioning from "***Broken to Repaired***," accept the healing in the process of change. God has to do an inner incision cutting away of waste. Think about it in this sense. The caterpillar enters the cocoon, unknowing of the change process. Biologically, we do not go through a metamorphosis as insects. The plan God originated for us, is in His image and in His likeness. Although our process is similar in terms of the growth from fetus to adulthood, we do not change from one thing to another. The caterpillar enters the cocoon and transforms into a butterfly. The change will create an entire different creature. A new outlook. A new appearance. A new form of existence. It trusts in the protection of its isolation period.

We process differently. From fetus to infant, to toddler, to young adult, to an adult, but still the same look, a human form of male and female. Our change is only from small to big. As the development of maturity takes place in you, God is able to transform you both internally, as well as externally. Spiritually, for that reason when you submit to the process of change it's an opportunity for growth. The bible says in 2 Corinthians 5:17, "***Therefore if any man be in Christ, he is a new creature: old things are passed away; behold, all things are become new.***"

Pick up the pieces and move forward. Live out the purpose God has ordained just for you. Do not allow a haughty ego to hold you back from transitioning from the broken place to the repaired you. Do not allow pride to show its head. The end of your destiny was designed by God before you were established on the earth. He said in this life that it would come a time you will be tried in tribulation that's difficult. Even during the times we are in now the pandemic has people losing hope. The perilous times are upon us! Nevertheless, JESUS is here to rescue you. Just believe that He is bringing us out victoriously!

Philippians 1:6 says: "***Being confident of this very thing, that*** *he which hath begun a good work in you will perform it until the day of Jesus Christ:"*

Through experience God began to show me that everything that I was going through was working in my favor. He was maturing me. You cannot continue to blame others for your failures. You must seek God to heal you and show you his plan. Although we all are challenged with some type of battle or weakness we are not ready to be buried yet?

Every day we have a chance to receive a given gift from the Lord. His grace and mercy will sustain you during the testing of the breaking process. So stand strong and walk in the promises that God has planned for your future. Frequently, many people look back and allow their past to immobilize them from moving into the promised place. A place that God has prepared for them. You are the light which will encourage others to hold on and keep the faith during their trying time. Let us remember to never look back on what caused your pain and refrain from hating that it happened to you. However, the experience will allow you to grow.

The response to what's going on and your reaction determines how long you will endure the chaos! Know this, the enemy can't change what God has promised you. He can only make you change your mind by distracting you with the pain that comes with the process of change, attempting to make you quit! I encourage you not to give in to his lies. He understands what he forfeited in life and now he wants to keep you from receiving the blessings of the Lord.

He knows what kind of life you will have and what rewards come with obeying God can bring. So just move forward and continue to believe that your obedience will be beneficial to you, your children, and your next generation. This is not the time to be spiritually buried yet. You must wait on the Lord and be cheerful in the waiting. satan wants you to abort your assignment for God.

You are sons and daughters of the most high God. We must yield in submission to our Father in heaven. We must give God all authority in our hearts, so that his glory may shine to the hearts of millions, delivering all that are oppressed. God needs our life to be an example before men, because it is he that has called us into righteousness and he shall work a perfect work in us. Believe it or not, in reading this book, you are entering into a covenant with the Father, submitting unto him and allowing him to order your steps.

After years of rejection, I thought it was all because of the spots that covered my face and body. IT wasn't that at all, but in essence, it was that I was "***Broken To Be Repaired!***" The name calling was as vicious as labeling the spots on my face as leopard spots. I have gotten past this level of criticism to some effect. Now I know that the spots don't define who God sees me as. They have only helped me grow into the individual I am now. He has placed me in a position to help those who have come across obstacles in the process of change. I truly am blessed and highly favored by the Lord who has kept not only my mind, but spared me from the hand of the enemy.

The indulgence of drug life and destructive path should have led me to the pits of hell, but God saved me and delivered me. God gave me hope in his word that allows me to stop seeking man's approval and accept the Christ that was within me to rise above unwanted thoughts that lead us into death. I thank God for He is a promise keeper. Even though we turn a deaf ear to God, He never leaves us. God is still faithful and forgives us of all our transgressions.

Remember the fiery trials come only to make us strong. The bible says "***Think it not strange concerning the fiery trials which is to try you as though some strange thing has happened unto you.***" (1 Pet. 4:12). It happened to me, but if we would admit it we've all been tested and tried in some area of our life. 1 Tim 2:3

says *"Thou therefore endure hardness as a good soldier of Jesus Christ."* **And** Psalm 34:19 says *"Many of the afflictions of the righteous, the Lord delivered him out of them all."* The word of God stands sure that He will never leave us alone. You are never, ever alone. The bible said He would be with us even until the end of the world.

We have to believe who the Bible says we are. Deuteronomy chapter 28 declares that we are the righteousness of God, the head and not the tail, blessed and not cursed, rich and not poor. Receiving all of these blessings, our mind must be transformed in order to receive who God says we are. In actuality, transformation of the mind has a waiting period. We must wait until God endows us with power from on high. We must wait on His anointing power, His grace, His mercy, His time, and His season to fulfil our destiny.

In Ecclesiastes 3:1(a) it says, **"To *everything there is a season, A time for every purpose under heaven:"*** King Solomon always talked about an appointed time; a future fulfillment that shall happen in our lives. This is the moment you don't want to miss. It is your **KAIROS** moment, which is a Greek term meaning an appointed time. In other words, I am speaking of your due season, your Now! This window of opportunity happens for us all and is sometimes overlooked by our blindness of the chaos going on around us. even during chaos, It's God's timing for your transformation and reward. This window of opportunity can open and close in such a short time frame. Therefore, you need to be aware of the movement of **KAIROS** time, or else you will miss out on something big God wants to do in your life. There are so many plans he wants to be fulfilled that concern you. Jesus said, " *The Lord Will Perfect that which concerneth me:"* (Ps. 138:8 a). God has promised us a life of pleasures. Oftentimes we must give up things that we believe to be best for us for his plan. The flesh is never willing, but we have to allow our minds to be transformed into the image of Christ. Then can we begin to win the war raging inside our heads. God said, *"For The Battle is not yours, but the Lord's."* (2 Chron. 20:15 b). Whether it's a spiritual or natural one.

Surely God knows our end from our beginning. Ecclesiastes 7:8 assures us,

"Better is the end of a thing than the beginning thereof: and the patient in spirit is better than the proud in spirit." Therefore, your patience will move the hand of God. David said, " *Wait on the LORD: be of good courage, and he shall strengthen thine heart: wait, I say, on the LORD." (*Ps. 27:14). God's timing will be the perfect time!

God created us with purpose in mind. We all must be changed in order to mature in the things of God. I reluctantly thought that in every place I worked it was a battlefield. Opposition is a never ending battle. But when we permit God to fight them, we win the war. In our struggles of life Ephesians 6:12 reminds us that "*We wrestle not against flesh and blood."* Let's take a closer look at Job's life. Job loses all that he had including his children. Instead of him becoming bitter or resentful he continues to praise God with the fruit of his lips. People mocked him and laughed about the boils infested all over his body. Through it all Job told the enemy, *"Though he slay me yet, will I trust Him."* (Job 13:15). When you understand that your praise moves God, you remain calm as you endure the hardships.

Even in Job's afflictions, he was faithful during his trial of testing. You must consider this, satan has to ask for permission from God before he can tempt you. As an observation, I see how one can become overwhelmed as God's testing and satan's tempting coincide with each other. However, God will allow satan to try and tempt us, only to try our faith for his restoration. In the amplified bible, 1 Corinthians 10:13 reassures us that, "*There hath no temptation taken you but such as is common to man: but God is faithful, who will not suffer you to be tempted above that ye are able; but will with the temptation also make a way to escape, that ye may be able to bear it."*

Nevertheless, after his suffering, Job expresses the sovereignty of God. He says, *"But he knoweth the way that I take when he has tried me, I shall come forth as gold!"* (Job 23:10).

Not only does Job praise God, but he also trusts him. He also encouraged himself in the Lord with the promise in Psalm 34:19 which says, *"Many are the afflictions of the righteous: but the LORD delivered him out of them all."* This Scripture is very encouraging. It should comfort you in knowing that no matter what you are going through you are going to come out. God released Job from captivity when he prayed for his friends. Not only did he pray for them, Job included his enemies too!! Not once did Job become filled with pride. He never blamed God instead, said, Lord, let your will be done in my life. When we yield to the will of God and stop covering up our flaws to criticize others we will discover our worth. I encourage you to see that it's just a test! God may seem to be silent at this point of your recovery, better yet, let me set your heart at ease. Jesus is your teacher. Now if you were in school, your literal teacher would not be conversing with you when you are testing. In fact she/he does not leave the room. Take consolation that Jesus is a *"Present Help,"* but quite during your testing trial of your faith.

Although you are challenged on every hand, God expects you to grow during the test. Remember it's not for bad, it's working for YOUR good! Winning the war is more profitable than winning the battle. If we could remain focused on the Sword which is the word of God we'd become victorious in all we set out to accomplish. Winning is not how strong you've become but in fact, how stable you are. Therefore, ***"Be ye steadfast and unmovable."*** (1Cor. 15:58). Set yourself like a rock and hold your ground so that the Lord God almighty can fight on your behalf.

You can't constantly give up because things don't go the way you plan. Father told us in His Word; ***"For my thoughts are not your thoughts, neither are your ways my ways, saith the Lord."*** (Isaiah 58:8). His are much greater. He said; *"But as it is written,* ***Eyes have not seen, ears have not heard; neither has it entered into the heart of man, the things which God has prepared for them that love Him."*** (1 Cor. 2:9). Strangely we would win the war if we'd stop fighting against ourselves. We are our greatest opponent. If our faith would line up with God's way, He'd shorten the battle.

Most times we aren't willing to give up the person or thing that God asked us to release. In order to attain the greater blessing, you must let go of the lesser. God promised that our latter would be greater than our beginning. The word of the Lord reads, "***Though thy beginning was small, yet thy latter end should greatly increase.***" (Job 8:7). Therefore, stand strong God has our due time strategically mapped out.

Let us take a look at Esther chapter 7 and how favor was found with the king and allowed her and the people to rise above Haman's intended demise. Queen Esther won not only the King favor, but freedom for her people. The battle is over and the war is won and we must realize who we are. I've won, and so have you. Victory took place on the cross at Calvary. We are above the enemy. Now the time has come for us to rise above the pit in pursuit of the palace.

In Genesis chapter 37 we find that Joseph was hated by his brothers and they cast him into a pit. Although they sought to get rid of him, God was with Joseph through every trial and test. You will be tried in many areas of your life. We are assured that the afflictions of God delivered upon us are not only that, but are stepping stones in a process for our betterment. Joseph never retaliates against them. In fact his love grew and in the end he delivered his brothers during the famine. Is this similar to your life?

We all know that Joseph was Jacob's favorite (daddy's pet). This placed him in a pit surrounded by haters. Many of the people around you see potential in you and begin to label you as an outcast. People tend to size you up with lies, persecution and rejection. These are all hard to cope with or contend with. Truly everyone wants to be accepted and loved.

Reality is when God has called you alone, you are purposed and a big part of His plan. You must accept the call or assignment. He called Abraham alone and blessed him only when he came in the perfect alignment and will of God. Abraham tried his way and didn't receive the promise until it totally lined up with God's plan. Both Joseph and Abraham endured a pit experience. We've all had a pit experience, ups and downs. When we want to throw in the towel and call it quits, we must realize who we are and what power God has given to us. We need to mature in our walk with him daily.

Romans 15:1 says *"WE then that are strong ought to bare the infirmities of the weak,"* therefore the pit transformed Joseph. The pit to the palace may sound frustrating, but it's a reality. You have all either been in a bad relationship that ended in divorce, financial low, battle of the flesh, whatever the challenge was God kept you from destruction.

A pit is the darkest place in your life. You must encounter a pit in order to attain entrance into the rest of God. Just as He told the children of Israel; *"I lead you through the wilderness to prove you and to prove what was in your heart..... to humble thee."* (Deut. 8:2 emphasis). We're in a process for change and repentance. We have to be molded into the image of Christ. God can do a quick work for us if we are willing to yield to the Holy Spirit.

Sometimes while we are in the pit it doesn't feel good to our flesh. Changes are uncomfortable. We are reassured through the word of God that to be transformed in our minds can change our circumstance. Joseph didn't fret because of the evil plot against him, so neither should we. **...... "All things work together for good."** (Rom.8:28)**." We know that** *"weeping may endure for a night, but JOY cometh in the morning!"* (Ps. 30:5).

I want you to know that you can survive through the breaking process and still live life as a victor. Everything that happened was for a purpose. You just read the scripture which declares that all things work together for your good. Listen, whatever process it took to get you to this point is beneficial. You are learning how to continue to believe that you can survive. I know some may have said you wouldn't make it. Nevertheless, you are here! As a matter of fact you are being healed and restored. I've come to realize that my past is behind me, but also it's a huge part of me. Every wrong turn, every bad decision, every choice I made has developed my character. Realize that we all have a purpose that's clothed with humility, God's grace, and his tender mercy will bring us through every trial and opposition. Let's face it, we all have had the pit experience and we are learning how to endure the process. Don't let your pain, hurt, and disappointments paralyze you from giving God the praise he deserves. Give God all the glory that is due to him! He inhabits our praises even in the most difficult times as these. Just be assured You are coming out into your season full of joy.

Prayer:

Lord, I thank you for giving me the strength to pick up the pieces of my life and move forward. Thank you for your directions and wisdom to understand and accept your will concerning my life. Help me to maintain my focus and stay on track. I am grateful for your unconditional love for me even during my rebellion seasons in my journey. I give you praise for keeping me safe through these perilous times. In Yeshua's name

Amen

SALVATION PRAYER:

Now is a good time to invite Jesus into your heart through the Salvation Prayer. He desires to have an intimate relationship with you. "*For God so loved the world that He gave us His only begotten son, Jesus that whoever believes in Him will not perish but have everlasting life*." (John 3:16). You must believe in your heart and then confess with your mouth that Jesus is the Son of God, and believe that He died for our sins and was raised from the dead, then you shall be saved. **Salvation** is a free gift to all who will accept Jesus in their heart. Ask him to repair the broken pieces of your life and make you whole. Read and confess this prayer of Salvation aloud;

Lord Jesus, I know that I have sinned and I ask for your forgiveness. I believe You died for my sins and rose from the dead. I believe you are ALIVE today. I repent and turn from my sinful ways and invite you into my heart. I make you Lord over my life, that I may live according to your will and plan for my life. I accept you as my Savior today, In Jesus name

Amen

DECLARE AND DECREE IN AGREEMENT

I admonish you to continue to Live out your purpose and fulfill your Destiny. Where you are **Healed** from the brokenness on your journey by being ***Repaired***, ***Revived, Refreshed***, and ***Restored***. I encourage you to make this declaration with me. Say this Aloud;

"LORD STRENGTHEN MY INNER MAN,
BY THE SPIRIT,
SO THAT MY FEELINGS, THOUGHTS, AND PURPOSE,
CAN BE PLACED MORE AND MORE,
UNDER YOUR INFLUENCE AND DIRECTIONS,
SO THAT THE SPIRIT CAN MANIFEST YOUR POWER,
THROUGH ME IN A GREATER MEASURE,
SO THAT I MAY EXPERIENCE BEING *"BROKEN TO BE REPAIRED,"*
AS PART OF MY PROCESS OF BECOMING WHOLE THROUGH YOUR
DIVINE HEALING,
BY THE BLOOD OF JESUS, YESHUA, OUR SAVIOR,
AMEN." *(by Annette Gatlin).*

CHAPTER EIGHT

AFFIRMATIONS
THAT AFFIRM

DECREE AND DECLARE

Here are five affirmations and ways to invoke the presence of God in your life.

1. Thank Him

Psalms 100 read; *"Make a joyful noise unto the Lord, all ye lands. Serve the Lord with gladness: come before his presence with singing. Know ye that the Lord he is God : it is he that has made us, and not we ourselves; we are his people, and the sheep of his pasture. Enter into his gates with thanksgiving, and into his courts with praise: be thankful unto him, and bless his name. For the Lord is good; his mercy is everlasting; and his truth endureth to all generations."*

2. Praise Him

Psalm 34:1-4 read, *"I will bless the Lord at all times: his praise shall continually be in my mouth. My soul shall make her boast in the Lord: the humble shall hear thereof and be glad. O magnify the Lord with me, and let us exalt his name together. I sought the Lord and he heard me, and delivered me from all my fears."*

3. Worship Him

John 4:23-24 read; *"But the hour is cometh and now is, when the true worshipers will worship the Father in spirit and in truth: for the Father is seeking such to worship Him. God is a Spirit, and those who worship Him must worship Him in spirit and in truth."*

4. Glorify Him

Revelation 4;11 read; " *Thou art worthy, O Lord, to receive glory and honour and power: for thou hast created all things, and for thy pleasure they are and were created.*

5. Rest In Him

Psalm 37:7 (a) read; *"Rest in the Lord, and wait patiently for him:*

In doing these five commands, your faith will be required. Do not stop daily chores or stand stagnant, but rather believe them even in the midst of suffering. In doing so, you will have divine healing. The healing that occurs when you totally rest in the Lord's presence. There comes a time when you must lay aside every hindrance that blocks the healing process for change. The wounds, the hurt, and the pain ends as you trust and fully give the Lord Jesus your confidence in Him and His word. Begin by affirming positive affirmations of who you are. Declare your next chapter as your healing continues every day. Here are some affirmations to get you started on your journey of being repaired.

MORNING Affirmations

- Lord, I give you Holy Reverence.
- I believe in Jesus Christ.
- I can do all things through Christ who strengthens me.
- I have the keys to the Kingdom of God.
- My ministry first begins in my home.
- I will meditate day and night upon the word of the Lord.
- I have the keys to the Kingdom of God.
- I am positive and confident.
- I will always give glory to God.
- I will pray earnestly for God's people with a sincere heart.
- I will encourage others.
- Whatever I do, I will do it as unto the Lord.
- I walk in Victory.
- I live life to the fullest.
- I am an encourager.
- I believe in myself.
- I have the wisdom and knowledge of God.
- My youth is renewed every day like an eagle.
- I live to declare the works of the Lord.
- I am the head and not the tail.
- I am blessed.
- My children are blessed.
- My home is blessed.
- Everything I set my hands to do prospers.
- God gives me witty ideas to produce wealth.
- I am wise.
- I walk in the favor of God.
- I have dominion to rule on the earth.
- The Earth opens up to me.
- Doors are open on my behalf.

WRITE YOUR MORNING AFFIRMATIONS:

1.

2.

3.

4.

5.

6.

7.

8.

AFTERNOON Affirmations

- I walk into a room and the atmosphere is changed.
- I am a leader.
- I am a lender.
- Men shall give into my bosom.
- I have whatsoever I say.
- My seed is greater than I am.
- The word of God operates fully in my life.
- My latter is greater than my past.
- I decree and declare a thing and it shall be established for me and my seed.
- Everywhere I go my territory is enlarged.
- I declare the works of the Lord.
- I have the tongue of a ready writer.
- I am Redeemed by Jesus' blood.
- I am strong in the Lord and the power of His might.
- I am Holy.
- I am light in a dark world.
- My body is the temple of the Living God.
- I am free from all sickness and disease.
- I am fearfully and wonderfully made by God.
- I am filled with the Holy Spirit.
- I am protected by angels.
- I am an encourager.
- I am healed and delivered.
- I am chosen by God.
- I guard the words of my mouth carefully.
- I am teachable.
- I know my worth.
- I have the wisdom of God.
- I am called by God.

- I am the apple of my God's eye.
- I am the salt of the earth.
- I am his beloved.
- I am rooted in Christ Jesus.
- I live my life in abundance.
- I have Victory in Jesus.
- I am more than a conqueror.
- I am committed to my purpose that God has given to me.
- I am on an assignment to win souls for Christ.
- I am loved, because I give love.
- I am special.
- I am positive.
- I am happy.
- I am kind.

WRITE YOUR AFTERNOON AFFIRMATIONS:

1.
2.
3.
4.
5.
6.
7.
8

NIGHT Affirmations

- I am confident.
- I am forgiving.
- I am brilliant.
- I believe in me.
- I have self control.
- I possess the fruits of the spirit.
- I am led by the Spirit of God.
- I am strong.
- I am brave.
- I have the mind of Christ.
- I am energetic.
- I am walking in the Overflow.
- I am a gift from God.
- I present my body to God as a Living Sacrifice everyday.
- Today is the best day of my life.
- I love myself.
- I love my children.
- I love the people of God.
- I attract positive people.
- I am successful.
- I have more than enough and enough to help others.
- I am funny.
- I show love everywhere I go.
- I compliment others.
- I am strong.
- I am living my best life through Jesus Christ.
- I am compassionate.
- I am understanding.
- I have patience.
- I am an overcomer.

- I am complete in Christ.
- I am faithful to God.
- I am living on purpose.
- I am armed for battle through prayer.
- I have the armor of God.
- My name is written in the Lamb's Book of Life.
- I proclaim the word of God.

WRITE YOUR NIGHT AFFIRMATIONS:

1.

2.

3.

4.

5.

6.

7.

8.

After making our affirmations I know that the Lord hears our cry for help and that he will answer our prayers when we are sincere. In the Bible, 2 Corinthians 12:9-10 makes it all clear as to how I survived the process of *"**Broken to be Repaired**"* It reads; *"**And he said unto me, My grace is sufficient for thee: for my strength is made perfect in weakness. Most gladly therefore will I rather glory in my infirmities, that the power of Christ may rest upon me. Therefore I take pleasure in infirmities, in reproaches, in necessities, in persecutions, in distresses for Christ's sake: for when I am weak, then am I strong.**"*

Prayer:

God I thank you as I have affirmed these declarations over my life that I walk circumspectly to your will. Lord help me to teach my children the ways of the Lord as I walk humbly before you. Let me be a light you have called out of the darkness to pull others to safety by your unconditional love you fill me with. I give you all the glory and honor to your name Jesus, I thank this day for restoration.

Amen

Comforting Scriptures

Psalm 138:8 read; *"The Lord will perfect that which concerneth me: thy mercy, O Lord endureth for ever: forsake not the works of thine own hands.*

Ephesians 3:20 read; *"Now unto him that is able to do exceeding abundantly above all that we ask or think, according to the power that worketh in us,"*

Jeremiah 29:11 read; *"For I know the thoughts that I think toward you, saith the Lord, thoughts of peace, and not of evil, to give you an expected end."*

Psalms 23:3 (a) read; *"He restoreth my soul:"*

CONCLUSION

*"**Broken To Be Repaired, A Guide For Healing Your Mind, Body, And Soul**"* is a must share with others you know are hurting or just in a place of isolation, or in fear of failing again. Now is a good time as any for you to pull on God for restoration. Things are no longer the same and during the pandemic we are able to see the hand of God healing, delivering, and repairing His people. As you continue your journey may it be an eye opener and a refreshing experience in finding your new. You will evolve in ways you never thought possible. In this season you can not allow the obstacles hidden to hinder your pursuit in the "***Broken To Be Repaired***" transformation. Take one step at a time, you can do this! During your transition you are leaving things behind that no longer causes you to grow. You will never be the same. Evaluation will help you see more clearly as you enter into the restored you. Never return to familiarity. It is time to launch out into the deep. Reach for more, Envision more, and Then go after your dreams. God is always present. Take this time to reflect and commune with God. As you do, be sure to seek His directions and listen for the still small voice as He speaks daily. The more you seek Him the more you will experience His presence. Promotion and transformation will propel you in the right path for God's divine direction for both you and the lives of your children and the generations to

come. And no matter what obstacles are placed in front of you during your process of being broken, accept what God allows, and do NOT give up. He has promised to be with you, even in the most difficult times. Your deliverance will help pull your brother/sister out their locked chamber of imprisonment of their mind. Once your vision is observed, not only will they be encouraged to run with it, they will rush to accomplish the task at hand. For the greater change within you, remember that you are called to complete certain missions that only you can fulfill. Although the Bee Hummingbird is the smallest bird of God's creation, they have great significance! The bird itself, **Is a small miracle** that gets nectar from the flower and then passes pollen to another one that causes pollination. They both Help each other. So we should be willing to help one another during our transformation.

God wants you to know the importance of how the smallest distraction of your life can hinder you. As they mean so much to Him in helping you get through it. You are His most valuable creation. So hum, sing as you will, shout if you must, whatever it takes to get you though this season. God supplies the smallest of birds with its necessities and He will supply for you as well. Be still and know that He is God. You are winning on every hand. God is turning around your downfall to an upgrade! God promised that our latter would be greater than our beginning. It starts here right now. I admonish you to do yourself the honor of releasing the things and people who caused the wound, hurt, or pain along your journey of soul revival and restoration. Pick up the pieces and finish your race. Things are being renewed as you continue your manifestation of miracles, signs, and wonders, as the Lord is working them out on your behalf. It is a new day now, so enjoy your transformation! **"BROKEN TO BE REPAIRED, A Guide For Healing Your Mind, Body, And**

Soul." Now prepare yourself by planning out your vision for the next season. I leave you with a most promising declaration over your life. The Lord has given us comfort in **Psalm 91**. Such an amazing and encouraging passage of Scripture that can help reassure our safety through the Blood of Jesus! It Passively read:

Psalms 91

1 "He that dwelleth in the secret place of the most High shall abide under the shadow of the Almighty.

2 I will say of the Lord, He is my refuge and my fortress: my God; in him will I trust.

3 Surely he shall deliver thee from the snare of the fowler, and from the noisome pestilence.

4 He shall cover thee with his feathers, and under his wings shalt thou trust: his truth shall be thy shield and buckler.

5 Thou shalt not be afraid for the terror by night; nor for the arrow that flieth by day;

6 Nor for the pestilence that walketh in darkness; nor for the destruction that wasteth at noonday.

7 A thousand shall fall at thy side, and ten thousand at thy right hand; but it shall not come nigh thee.

8 Only with thine eyes shalt thou behold and see the reward of the wicked.

9 Because thou hast made the Lord, which is my refuge, even the most High, thy habitation;

10 There shall no evil befall thee, neither shall any plague come nigh thy dwelling.

11 For he shall give his angels charge over thee, to keep thee in all thy ways.

12 They shall bear thee up in their hands, lest thou dash thy foot against a stone.

13 Thou shalt tread upon the lion and adder: the young lion and the dragon shalt thou trample under feet.

14 Because he hath set his love upon me, therefore will I deliver him: I will set him on high, because he hath known my name.

15 He shall call upon me, and I will answer him: I will be with him in trouble; I will deliver him, and honour him.

16 With long life will I satisfy him, and shew him my salvation."

Prayer:

*Father, we thank you for your son **Jesus and His blood sacrifice**. Lord, we thank you for your divine protection and peace for our hearts and minds. **Father** we ask, that you will continue to direct our paths and make our crooked ways straight. Teach us how to hear your voice clearly. We thank you for your grace and mercy that stayed on the hand of our enemy over our life. Lord we render our hearts to you and we ask that you forgive us of all our unrighteousness and sinful ways. Purge us that we may grow in your wisdom and knowledge. Keep our minds that we may not enter into temptation that would cause us to fail you. **Father,** I pray that you will bless every reader of this book. Encourage their hearts to stay in the race and never give up. Lead them to the rock, strengthen them with your delivering power, and save them so they are healed from every wound, hurt and pain in their life that may come. Prepare them for this miracle breakthrough and divine **CHANGE** as they submit to your will and plan for their lives! Thank you for this incredible encouragement from **"BROKEN TO BE REPAIRED"** only by You Lord, in **Jesus** name,*

Amen

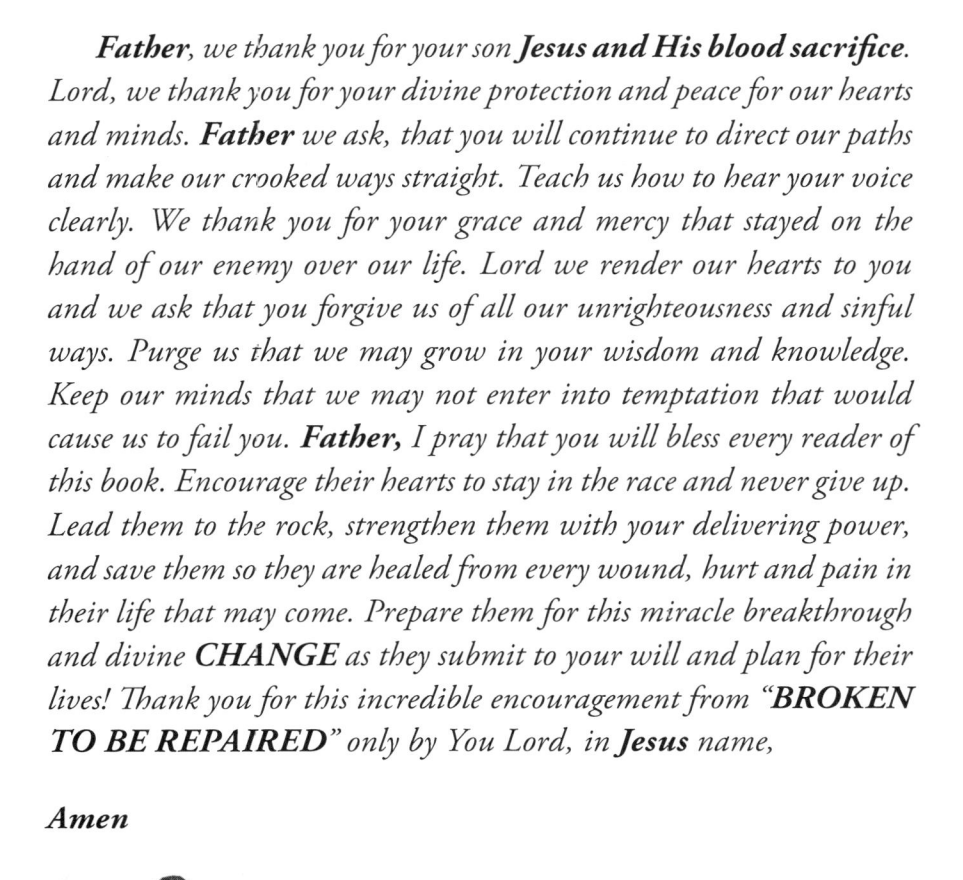

REFERENCES

ENDNOTES

1. Wilma Rudolph Quotes. (n.d.). BrainyQuote.com. Retrieved September 4, 2020, from BrainyQuote.com https://www.brainyquote.com/quotes/wilma_rudolph_184353

2. Wound. 2020. In Dictionary.com.Retrieved from: https://.www.dictionary.com

3. Pain. 2020. In Merriam-Wesber.com. Retrieved from: https://www.merrism-webster.com/dictionary/pain

4. Hyman, P. (2015). Aphorisms and Editions: What Exactly Did Brillat-Savarin Say? *Petitis Propos Culinaires, 103*, 22-30.

5. Hurt. 2020. In Merriam-Webster.com. Retrieved from: https://www.merrism-webster.com/dictionary/hurt

6. Merriam-Webster. (n.d.). Hurt. In Merriam-Webster.com dictionary. Retrieved October 8, 2020, from https://www.merriam-webster.com/dictionary/hurt

7. Retrieved From: Wikipedia, The Free Encyclopedia. https://en.m.wikipedia.org/wiki/Watchman_Nee

8. Nee, Watchman. Christian Quotes. (July, 27, 2014). Retrieved from: www.christianquotes.info.

9. Vince Lombardi Brainy Quotes. (n.d.).BrainyQuote.com. Retrieved August 4, 2020, from BrainyQuote.com

Website:https://www.brainy.com/quotes/vince_lombardi_
122285

10. Wilma Rudolph Quote. (n.d.). BrainyQuote.com. Retrieved
    August 4, 2020, from BrainyQuote.com Website:
    https://www.brainyquote.com/quotes/wilma_rudolph_
    184355

11. Norwood, Arlisha."Wilma Rudolph." National Women's
    History Museum. National Women's History Museum,
    2017. Date accessed.
    Retrieved from:
    www.womenshistory.org/education-resources/biographies/
    wilma-rudolph.

12. All Scriptures quotations, unless otherwise indicated, are
    taken from King James Version.

13. The Author makes emphasis and paraphrases with some
    scriptures throughout the book.

14. The Author intentionally used lower case for the name of
    satan.

SCRIPTURE INDEX

Old Testament

- Genesis 1:26-27; 19:26; 29:17-35; 37; 49:29
- Exodus
- Leviticus
- Numbers
- Deuteronomy 8:2; 30:19
- Joshua
- Judges
- Ruth
- 1 Samuel
- 2 Samuel
- 1 Kings
- 2 Kings
- 1 Chronicles
- 2 Chronicles 20:15
- Ezra
- Nehemiah 8:10
- Esther 7
- Job 13:15; 23:10
- Psalms 4:4; 17:8; 15:12; 23:3; 30:5; 34:1-4; 34:19; 37:7; 37:23-24; 91:1-16; 100; 115:12; 138:8
- Proverbs 3:6; 3:11-12; 27:17
- Ecclesiastes 3:1; 3:11; 4:9

- Song of Solomon
- Isaiah 30:21; 61:3; 64:8
- Jeremiah 1:5; 18:3-4; 18:6; 29:11
- Lamentations
- Ezekiel
- Daniel
- Hosea
- Joel
- Amos
- Obadiah
- Jonah
- Micah
- Nahum
- Habakkuk 2:2
- Zephaniah 3:17
- Malachi

New Testament

- Matthew
- Mark 9:23
- Luke 15; 19:10
- John 4:23-24; 10:10; 14:6; 15:7; 16:21
- Acts 4:12
- Romans 5:3-5; 8:28; 8:37; 15:1; 15:4; 15:58
- 1 Corinthians 2:9; 5:17; 9:24-27; 10:13
- 2 Corinthians 5:17; 12:9-10
- Galatians 2:20
- Ephesians 2:10; 3:20; 6:10; 6:12
- Philippians 1:6; 4:13
- Colossians
- 1 Thessalonians

- 2 Thessalonians
- 1 Timothy 2:3; 2:13
- 2 Timothy
- Titus
- Philemon
- Hebrews 5:8-10; 11:6; 12:1-2; 13:8
- James
- 1 Peter 2:12; 4:12-13; 5:10
- 2 Peter
- 1 John
- 2 John
- 3 John
- Jude
- Revelation 4:11

NOTES

NOTES

NOTES

NOTES

ABOUT THE AUTHOR

As an Evangelist, Founder and CEO of Destined For Greatness International Ministry, Ordained Elder, Master Cosmetologist, and Mother-Annette Gatlin balances family life and ministry with grace, wisdom, and tenacity. Known for her exuberant style of preaching and praise, Evangelist Gatlin has traveled extensively and has been dedicated to evangelism for more than 23 years. She preachers as Paul proclaimed; "My speech and my preaching is not with the enticing words of man's wisdom, but that it is in the demonstration of the Holy Spirit and Power of God." (1

Corinthians 2:4, with emphasis). That we all can encounter the presence of the Lord.

As a nationally sought after speaker at conferences and churches, Gatlin is a highly respected Woman of God and her reputation stands firmly in the experiences of those she has come into contact with. She was blessed to share ministry with her husband, the late Bishop Charles Edward Gatlin. Together they founded Destined for Greatness International Ministry October 8, 2008. Recently, thereafter, God has given her charge of a women's ministry, Wings of Beauty Outreach for Broken Women which originated in 2012.

As a hairstylist for 37 years, Evangelist Gatlin's passion to beautify and uplift others remains evident as she volunteers her professional services. She has served as a Bible reader, prayer warrior, consultant, and hairstylist for various nursing homes throughout Georgia, Tennessee, and Arkansas.

Evangelist Gatlin has obtained a BA in Communications/Culture from the University Of Phoenix, an Associates in Biblical Studies from Covenant Theological Seminary, and an Associates Degree in Speech and Theatre at Austin Peay State University.

She is the host of The Clarion Call featured on Facebook Live and a nationwide conference call that occurs on a weekly occasion. Among her accolades, Evangelist Gatlin feels that her most rewarding accomplishments are those of the significant roles she plays in her family. She is a loving mother of four beautiful children and Nana of 6 grandchildren. She truly believes your ministry begins in your home.

As a woman of many talents and anointing, she is able to be used by God as a martyr and a testament to his grace and mercy. Gatlin now uses her story as a way to empower women around the nation and bring them the inevitable truth, established by

God, that they are women of beauty, strength, and triumphant accomplishments.

God has anointed Evangelist Gatlin to operate under the powerful influential calling of John the Baptist. God has commissioned her to bellow and to preach his unadulterated word with fire from the Holy Spirit. Her mission is to call sin hindered souls to repent and be transformed into the pure vessels God needs for his kingdom and to set the captive free.

Gatlin's main focus is to encourage the lost, broken, and despairing, to stand up and live boldly. In hopes that they fulfill their divine purpose. As a survivor of degenerate bone disease, rape, alcohol, drugs, rejection, and domestic violence, Gatlin's testimony is one that will make you laugh, cry, and acknowledge the truth in God's **DIVINE RESTORATION**. Gatlin's mission is to establish confidence in those who are wounded as she divulges their intended purpose in God and discover their true identity in Him.

To Contact Evangelist Annette Gatlin's Ministry, visit:

webpage: www.destinedforgreatnessinternational.org
Facebook: Annette Hines-Gatlin
Instagram: cinderrellawon
Instagram: lady_gatlin
Twitter: @edwardgatli

Address:
1443 Rock Spring Road
Suite 9
Bel Air, MD
21014

Email address – wingsofbeauty737@gmail.com